G000150670

Dete
The Urban Shepherd

To my saviour "Patch" Jones. enjoy!. Neville Sprague "Detective Deville"

Detective Deville
The Urban Shepherd

The hilarious memoirs of a
London Policeman

ivor M bundell

THE CHOIR PRESS

Copyright © 2022 ivor M bundell

All rights reserved. No part of this publication may be
reproduced or transmitted in any form or by any means,
electronic or mechanical including photocopying, recording or
any information storage or retrieval system, without prior
permission in writing from the publishers.

The right of ivor M bundell to be identified as the author of this
work has been asserted by him in accordance with the
Copyright, Designs and Patents Act 1988

First published in the United Kingdom in 2022 by
The Choir Press

ISBN 978-1-78963-246-0

Cover Design & Artwork by Jim LeCouteur
https://www.devilletruecrime.co.uk

For more information about other works by Ivor see:
www.bundellbros.co.uk

ivor M bundell

Dedication

This book is dedicated to a very unusual and resourceful detective, Archie Gemmell.

Archie solved many difficult cases using his skills to blend into undercover, covert operations. His tenacity was legendary and, for the most part, only known about by a few during his career. His work was often very secret, extremely dangerous and highly pressurised.

Archie was, of course, assisted by his "cricket" (*gryllidae*) called Clive.

Contents

Reward   ix

Preface   xii

A Policeman's Best Friend   1

The Invisible Cyclist   5

Mr Sayed Sadha's Carpet Emporium & Oriental Bazaar   10

A Metropolitan Mystery Tour   15

On the Other Side of the Street   21

The Royal Parks Policeman or The One That Got Away   24

The St Pancras Pantomime   27

The Columbo of Kensington   29

The Earls Court Hue & Cry   32

A Crime-Fighter's Career   35

Human Nature   40

What's in a Name?   45

A Twist of Fate   47

In Coram's Fields   52

A Tabloid Tale   54

Given A Chance   60

Operation Seaside   64

On Interviewing Considered as One of the Fine Arts   73

Pandora's Box   77

A Bad Business in Brighton   84

Cards, Capers and Collections 88

Curlers 95

Colwyn Bay Calling 100

The Grand Piano 106

The Good Samaritans 111

Confession of a Master Car Thief 114

Archie and the Cricket 121

Gorilla Tactics 125

The London Village of Melsham (Part 1) 129

The London Village of Melsham (Part 2) 133

The London Village of Melsham (Part 3) 137

A Visit to Melsham 142

Acknowledgements 146

Reward

All the stories in this collection are true. Well, not quite. There is a single exception, which is *true-to-life*. Perhaps you could employ your own DeVille-like skills of observation and detection in order to identify which particular story this is?

A special reward is offered, a bottle of the finest single malt whisky, for the first correct answer drawn from a hat at a date to be decided (see blog). The tie-breaker will be, in no more than forty words, why you especially liked a particular story.

The prize will be presented by DeVille in person at the *Pig & Whistle*, London.

Preface

The overall structure of these stories is that of a patchwork quilt with patterns that are sometimes repeated and juxtaposed or complementary and, more often than not, downright odd. DeVille himself defines his own method as being a bit like a pinball machine where one thought sparks off another and then another idea blazes into view redirecting the trajectory of his tale. Let me explain how we went about capturing these stories and how we proceeded to shape and polish them.

DeVille and I agree that merely recording him as he narrates a story does not capture all that the *live* experience offers. We try to recreate the occasion of the story as it is told, as well as the story itself. It is sometimes necessary for me, as the writer, to check key facts with DeVille. On other occasions DeVille will correct my misunderstanding or omission of key facts. In either case, it is a two-way process of carefully listening to and respecting each other's position. I am acutely aware of being a curator of DeVille's tales. He is equally aware that his stories need to work well in written form. Both of us recognise the need to convey as accurately as possible the nature of the narrative experience.

However, each story is different. Sometimes we 'to-and-fro' a bit before arriving at the final result but other times a single telling is enough. We are looking for authenticity rather than literal accuracy, trying to recapture the original experience.

As well as the exchange between DeVille as the source and myself as the writer, there is a third party involved: You, the reader. Or very often the pilot reader. We try out the stories on a few friendly victims to see how they respond. Many of these pilot readers have heard the stories told in person by DeVille and recognise them.

One observation struck me as worthy of a response. Could the stories be ordered to follow the chronology of DeVille's career? In response I have written a piece entitled *A Crime-Fighter's Career* which, I hope, addresses this point.

It remains to be seen how we proceed to publication but,

whatever the outcome, I feel privileged to have had the opportunity to tell someone else's stories, stories that have been generously shared with me and many others. I hope I have done justice to them and to DeVille himself. If not then I console myself with the thought that I shall one day receive my summons to the *Final Court of Appeal* where I shall be obliged to answer for my sins.

A Policeman's Best Friend

*I have never known why some of us walk on four legs and
others walk on just two. It seems strange to me. I've always
used four. I have a tail, of course. Sometimes those with four
legs have no tail. But I do. You can be sure though that the
dogs with two legs never have a tail. Oh yes, they will
sometimes go round and round in circles but it's not because
they're chasing their tail. I used to like chasing my tail but I've
grown out of that now. I used to like chasing cats but now I
prefer chasing other dogs, especially the two-legs.*

"I was partnering Saunders that day. He was, as usual, dressed
immaculately. I had polished my shoes over the weekend and was
a match for him in the shoe department, on that occasion at least.
We arrived at the address we had been given. It was an
anonymous road in West Acton, much like others in the vicinity.
We parked round the corner and briefly rehearsed our piece. As
we approached No. 80 Clanford Crescent we were greeted by a
large Alsatian dog. It turned and scratched at the front door; it
seemed to be asking to be let it in. We rang the doorbell."

'Marge, can you get that please,'
cried Henry from the attic where he
was working on the new track layout
for his model railway. It was based on
the junction between the mainline and
the disused section that extended as far
as Norton Bridge.

'It's the police, Henry, they want to
come in.'

'Okay, I'll be down in just a minute.'
Henry assumed they must have come in
response to the report he had made
about some tools that had gone missing
from the garden shed, including an
electric hedge-trimmer.

DeVille raised his hat politely and
Mrs Reardon invited the officers in. As

she unchained the door, a large dog brushed past her into the house before she had had time to utter any exclamation of surprise. The two officers followed immediately, dutifully wiping their feet on the doormat as they entered. She ushered them into the front parlour.

'Henry will be down in just a moment. Can I offer you a cup of tea?' Mrs Reardon enquired.

"That would be nice," I said, "White with two sugars. And the same for my colleague, please." Saunders never drank tea but together they had established this standard response to avoid complications.

I explored all around the living-room, especially behind the sofa. I found an old dry biscuit and two sweet wrappers. I felt sure I could smell something more interesting but I couldn't quite place it. Perhaps it was a faint trace of rabbit? I wasn't sure but it seemed vaguely familiar.

Henry appeared at the door to the living room.

'Good afternoon, gentlemen. Good news is it?' He saw that the police had brought reinforcements with them. An Alsatian was sitting with its back to the fireplace, facing him as he stepped into the room. It wagged its tail and looked from him to the two officers who had stood up.

'Do please sit down. No standing on ceremony. As I was saying – do you have any news?'

"I let Saunders take the lead on this as it had been his collar. Mrs Reardon reappeared at the doorway carrying a tray laden with crockery and cakes. I got up straightaway and offered to assist, clearing a space on the occasional table in the corner of the room, nearly tripping over the dog in the process."

I decided to sit down on the rather fine goatskin rug placed invitingly in front of the open fireplace. It was a good spot, even on a warm day like today when the fire remained unlit. I watched and listened carefully as tea was served. One of the policemen, the shorter one I think, tripped over my tail. Almost stood on it in fact! No respecters of tails these two-leggers, I tell you.

"Saunders seemed to be wrapping things up and I had finished my tea. Mr and Mrs Reardon seemed pleased with the conclusion to matters."

'Another cake?' Mrs Reardon offered temptingly.

'Now come on Marg, we mustn't keep these officers any longer. I'm sure they've got work to do!'

"As a matter of fact we had, but it was only paperwork and neither of us were thrilled at the prospect."

As no-one had offered me a piece of cake I decided I should go and see what might be hidden behind the armchair in the corner of the room, just under the three plaster ducks hanging on the wall and next to the fern plant on a wooden stand. I carefully avoided the plant and began to search for anything interesting I could find.

"We had completed our enquiries and were getting ready to leave. Then the Alsatian appeared from behind an armchair, turned two circles, and deposited a large dog poo on Mrs Reardon's carpet.

I looked at Saunders who grimaced. We got up to leave but Mrs Reardon did not look at all pleased. She nudged her husband with her elbow saying: 'You need to say something to them!' Then Mr Reardon said:

'What are you going to do about that?' pointing to the offending and aforementioned evidence.

'Why do you want *us* to do something about it, Mr Reardon?' I asked.

'Well it's your bloomin' dog, isn't it?' replied Mr Reardon.

I looked at Mr Reardon. Mr Reardon looked at me. I looked at Saunders and Saunders looked at Mr Reardon. The dog looked at the floor.

'No, it's your dog,' I said.

'Oh no it isn't!' said Mr Reardon. 'It came in with you and your colleague.'

'It just followed us in, it's not ours' replied Saunders.

'Oh yes it is!'"

It was at this point that I realised my police career was now hanging in the balance. Still, it was good to be a police dog, even if it was only for a short while. At last the front-door was opened and I dashed out of the room and past the two policemen as fast as I could.

"As we reached the front gate we saw the Alsatian bound up to a man; he was barking and wagging his tail in greeting – the dog that is, not the man."

'So there you are! Now where've you been? What've you been up to?' asked the man as he reciprocated the dog's delighted greeting.

"And now I watch, without saying a word, as Saunders approaches the pair and commences what must be a tactful interview, undertaken by himself as a uniformed representative of the Law:

'Good afternoon, Sir. Is this dog yours, by any chance?'

'Well, yes, he is. This is Rover.'

'Yes, we're already well acquainted, Sir. I am obliged to inform you that your dog is required to wear a collar at all times and to be kept on a lead in public.'

'Why yes, of course. I'm afraid he was in the garden and must have got loose somehow. I'll put him on the lead straightaway.'

'Oh and just one other thing, Sir,' said Saunders, without missing a beat and keeping a perfectly straight face.

'Certainly, what's that?'

'I believe this belongs to you, Sir?' and so saying he handed the man a doggie-poo bag.

A couple of weeks later I was queuing for lunch in the police canteen and bumped into Noakes, the police-dog handler:

'I hear we are now using plain clothes police-dogs!' he said.

'That's right', I answered, '*Saunders idea, of course!*'"

The Invisible Cyclist

I was still at school when DeVille began his career as a young bobby on the beat in Holborn, London. I would not move to London for another three years and I would not leave London for another six. At the end of my last year in London I would take the bus from the East End to Holborn every day for a month. .

Very near the stop where I got off was the beat that DeVille had patrolled some years before. This was New Oxford Street, running to the East of the infamous Centre Point building. The pavements told me no stories then but now I hear voices, and the echoes of voices, none clearer than that of DeVille himself, an honest man among rogues and villains.

It must have been late November or early December. It was dark despite the street lights and the Christmas lights in Oxford Street had been turned off for the night. It was gone midnight and the traffic was thinning out, West End theatre-goers were home by now, and there were only a few late-night revellers still about. Meanwhile homeless people were constructing their make-shift cardboard houses in the shadow of Centre Point and settling down for another damp and miserable night.

First Night- Introductions

"I first noticed him when he turned the corner into Jermyn Street. He was cycling upright. He did not seem to be in a hurry but neither was he dawdling along."

So DeVille described his first encounter with the mysterious cyclist. It was merely another routine encounter on an otherwise uneventful night. Something to keep him awake if not unduly alert. He stepped off the pavement under the light of a street lamp and held up his hand, signalling to the cyclist to halt.

"You do not appear to have any lights."

"No? The battery, she is flat, *si*?

DeVille noticed the accent and discovered the cyclist worked as a waiter in the West End. He was on his way home to Hackney.

"Well, make sure you get a battery. I don't want to find you splattered all over the road just because some driver didn't see you coming!"

"Ok, ok, I do this."

"Now push your bike along. Off you go.

"*Si, si*. No problem."

And he walks off a few paces and then jumps on his bike and pedals away *multo furioso*!

DeVille turned and continued, philosophically, on his vigil.

Second Night – Nerves

"Hello, hello," I said, as I accosted our lamp-less cyclist the following night.

"Did you really say that?" I asked.

"Why not?" replied DeVille, "I'm a policeman, aren't I?"

Clearly he enjoyed the role he played. If he was going to be a policeman then he would act the part. No point in pretending to be anything else. Besides, it was like a part of his uniform. It gave him credibility and authority. People knew where they stood. Well, most people. Perhaps our cyclist was the exception.

"I felt it was my duty to uphold the law. No cycling without lights. But what was the best thing to do in terms of helping this cyclist's welfare? What was best for him? So I let down his tyres. That way he couldn't put himself in danger.

Now he would have to push his bike home. He seemed resigned to his fate. However, about a hundred yards down the road our resourceful cyclist takes a pump out of his sleeve, waves it about, and says he's going to pump them up again! I didn't bother to give chase. I knew I'd have another chance to assist him."

Third Night – Nothing to Report

"Of course, as you can imagine, by the third night I was on the lookout. I lay in wait like a coiled spring, ready to pounce like a Bengal tiger, ready to scare him out of his wits."

So DeVille began his description of the third night of his active vigil: monitoring the safety of the London public in general and a certain London cyclist in particular.

"So did you run across the cyclist on the third night? What happened?" I asked.

"Well no, as a matter of fact I didn't. I thought perhaps it might have been his night off or maybe he'd taken a different route home on this occasion."

"Were you disappointed?" I asked.

"No, not disappointed exactly – I wouldn't say that – but I realised I might have to bide my time. I always like to take the long view. I believe justice comes to those who wait. I did a lot of waiting in those days. It was the lot of a humble bobby. I was there to be seen, to provide a sense of security to anyone out and about late at night. Clearly my mission was unappreciated by our *Giro D'Italia* hopeful. He seemed to look upon my presence as a nuisance at best and as a menace at worst."

"So what happened the next night?" I enquired.

Fourth Night – The Side-Street Shuffle

"I'd had the rest of the following day and the early part of the evening to reflect on matters. I would take a different approach tonight, quite literally. I reckoned that, if he was heading back to Hackney from the West End, there was another route he might take in an attempt to bypass me on my standard beat. Tonight I would go off-beat. Take a syncopated approach. Be unpredictable."

As DeVille explained his strategy to me, I listened with eager anticipation of tonight's encounter.

"Well, this time I surprises our invisible cyclist with a crafty interception at the pedestrian bollards on the north side of Grays Inn."

"So what did you say this time?" I asked.

"Well, it's not so much what I said as what I did."

DeVille paused to light another cigar, though there was already one half-smoked resting on the edge of the ashtray. He refilled his glass with dry white wine and continued:

"So what did you do?" I asked.

"What would you have done? This fellow had made no effort to heed my advice or comply with the law. I could have nicked him, of course, but that would have meant unnecessary paperwork. Sometimes you have to use your initiative in these situations."

"Okay so what initiative did you use on this occasion?" I prompted.

"Quite simple really. I removed the valves from the tyres. No way he was going to cycle home then!"

"So you made your point pretty clear," I observed.

"Yes, I suppose you could say that," said DeVille.

"So this time he did have to walk home?"

"That's right."

Fifth Night – An Understanding

"Anyway, by this time the whole scenario was beginning to feel bit like an old 78 rpm record stuck on a gramophone," said DeVille.

"Well, I like the tune it's playing. Can I hear it again?"

"Ok. So this time I trusted to luck. I didn't plan an ambush or try to anticipate his route. If he came my way again, fine. I would let chance or fate play its part."

"I never took you for someone who would trust to luck!"

"No, I suppose not but on this occasion it seemed appropriate enough. Anyway, we did indeed bump into each other again – almost literally. He had no light and I was stepping off the pavement and onto the road."

"So what did you do?"

"Well, I let down his tyres again, removed his valves, threw them down the drain, and sent him on his way. But he was learning!"

"What do you mean," I asked.

"He had a set of spare valves on him! And then he produces a front-lamp from his bag and puts it on the handlebars. We both just stood there and laughed!"

"So what then?"

"Well, I helped him fix his bike, of course!"

Sixth Night – Finale

"The next night I was surprised by my cyclist as he approached head on with all lights ablaze and wearing a hi-vis fluorescent yellow jacket. He stopped to greet me like an old friend and proudly showed off his latest gear. He even had a lamp attached to his forehead like a cave explorer. I have to admit I felt proud of my unlikely accomplice.

It was only a couple of weeks later that a young lad was knocked down and killed in High Holborn. It was past midnight and he was riding without lights. He never gave himself a chance. You can't blame the bus driver."

Mr Sayed Sadha's Carpet Emporium & Oriental Bazaar

Every morning DeVille would make his way to work using a slightly different route. This was not a matter of security, although there was a threat from the IRA at the time, but rather a routine that he had begun to cultivate simply because he preferred it. He found it tedious to follow the same route every day.

This is what he told me and I had no reason to question him. Well, not on this matter at least. For the time being let us follow him on one of these routes, one which took him past the *Sayed Sadha Carpet Emporium and Oriental Bazaar (London, Hyderabad, and New York)* located in Southwark. This was before the reconstruction of the *Globe Theatre* and the *Tate Modern*. It was still a warren of streets in which you might easily get lost. I only remember the area from the time construction first started on the new *Globe*; I was working in the back-office of a major American Bank which has since ceased to exist. Something about fraudulent trading, I believe. I mentioned this to DeVille. He said nothing but simply raised a querulous eyebrow. But I should let DeVille tell this story; after all, it is his to tell, not mine.

"I'd met Sayed a few times. We would say hello as he stood outside his Emporium and smoked an early morning cigarette and I walked along a small road south of the Thames towards London Bridge. He knew I was in the force. He didn't know exactly where I was based or what I did – it was murders, at that time. I was in what the Yanks would call the *Homicide Team*. We called it the *Murder Squad* – 'cause most days we could murder a cup of tea! Anyway, one day Sayed hailed me and asked if he could have a quick word. It was an opportunity to get to know him better and, naturally, I was curious."

"Ah Mr Deevil, Sah! Come, I am needing to talk most heartily with you now. Please take tea, Sah. With me now."

"Well, I was in no hurry to return to a pile of paperwork. Why do today what you can happily put off till tomorrow, that's what I say. Anyway, I agreed to his offer of a mug of tea: two sugars, with milk. Turned out to be sugar with three-fingers of tea and some warm milk. Still, I was happy to adjust to his customary take on our national drink; after all, it was his before it was mine."

DeVille opened another bottle and offered me a refill. I accepted. A fine Chilean Chardonnay, good value.

"Sayed explained he had been losing stock from his warehouse but could not see how it was disappearing. He detected no pilfering and the main items seemed to be rugs and carpets – objects not readily removed without somebody seeing something. I listened to what he had to say and promised I'd look into it for him. I'd just about finished my tea so I said goodbye and said I'd call in again later that week, or early next week. He seemed happy that I had offered to help."

DeVille picked up his lighter and seemed to study it, as if it were an object of some value or perhaps a piece of evidence.

I asked him if it was a present.

"What this? Yes, Sayed gave it to me. Sort of a reward. I think of it as a memento really. Not supposed to accept gifts, of course. Might be misconstrued as a bribe or something, I suppose. Anyway, he gave it to me, after the event."

I knew that DeVille was as honest as the day etc. Nobody could possibly link him with corruption of any kind. But I also knew that the time in which he worked as an officer of the law was a time in which corruption was rife. Whether this was merely because investigative journalism was able to sniff it out and blow it up out of all proportion, or it was the truth, I do not know. Whatever, DeVille himself was what, in the old-fashioned term, you would call 'an honest copper' – more than that, he was an honest man.

"It wasn't a reward really; I had no expectation of anything when I offered to help him. It was, in a way, just a friendly gesture. Of course I meant to help him, if I could, but it was not in expectation of any reward. Nothing was offered in payment up-front – not unless you think a mug of tea is a bribe!"

I did not.

"It was a couple of weeks before I saw Sayed again. I had been working on a big bank robbery and then been away in Norfolk investigating a lead. And there was all the paperwork to do, of course."

"So what happened when you next saw Sayed?" I asked.

"Well, it was by accident actually. I was on my way home after work one evening. I had been working late, catching up in the paperwork. I dropped into the *Pig and Whistle* – just for a quick pint and to see how Louise, the new owner of the pub, was getting on. Lovely lady, widow of one of my old colleagues at the Met. He died of cancer, I'm sorry to say. Anyway, Sayed was sitting on his own at a table over in the corner. He didn't notice me but I saw him and went over to say hello, conscious of the fact I hadn't kept my promise to him. He seemed happy to see me. His glass was nearly empty. I offered to get him another orange juice and he accepted."

"Most glad it is I am to see you Mr Deevil," he said, "I am needing assistance of the utmost urgency!"

DeVille brought the drinks back to the table and sat down.

"Okay, so tell me, what's the trouble Sayed."

Sayed Sadha, of the *S.S. Carpet Emporium and Oriental Bazaar (London, Hyderabad, and New York)* began to explain his most perturbed and necessary consternation:

"I am losing the money of my carpets that are missing, you see. It is the most upsetting!"

Clearly Sayed was very distressed about his losses and DeVille vowed to help.

"Okay Sayed, I'll drop by tomorrow, later on in the afternoon. Let's say about four o'clock. I'm sure we can sort this out."

Having given Mr Sadha some degree of reassurance, DeVille himself hoped he would be able to live up to his promise. Usually confident of and in his own abilities he felt the slightest tremor of self-doubt on this particular occasion, as if somewhere a huge shelf of ice had slipped into the sea and set in motion a wave that, though it might take time to arrive, would inevitably reach shore and wreak havoc. He hoped he hadn't made a promise he couldn't keep.

At four-thirty precisely, on the afternoon of Thursday the twenty-third, Detective Sergeant DeVille and D.S. Sanders arrived at the aforementioned if somewhat obscure S.S. Carpet Emporium and Oriental Bazaar (London, etc.) in Southwark, in a small road parallel to Stafford St. DeVille continues:

"Sayed greeted us at the door. I sent Saunders to survey the warehouse from the outside – get a feel for its location and proximity to other roads and buildings. I followed Sayed into the warehouse. It was dimly lit but clearly contained a vast quantity of goods. Mostly it was boxes and pallets and rolls of brightly coloured oriental material. We stopped as Sayed turned to face me. He began to explain that it appeared he was losing only the most beautiful of Persian rugs, transported by camel over the desert and then by privately sponsored freight from Dubai to Amsterdam. It was then that I saw a carpet, more precisely a flying carpet. I had never seen a flying carpet before and had certainly not expected to do so on this occasion. But that's what I saw, believe me!"

We must all have looked slightly puzzled as DeVille continued:

"Yes, a flying carpet. No one on board, mind you. A Persian carpet, rolled tight as a Cuban cigar, just then made its maiden flight from East to West, across the aisle, and out through the porthole of the S.S. Carpet Emporium and Oriental Bazaar into the street below. And as Saunders later informed me, onto the flatbed of a waiting truck below."

DeVille said nothing. He carefully maintained his composure so as not to alarm Mr Sayed Sadha in any way and so as not to alarm the putative perpetrator. He suspected the mystery was about to be solved but wanted to be sure of the facts. Besides, he had not seen the method by which the aforementioned carpet had been launched, propelled, and flighted through the open window and into the street below.

"I indicated to Sayed to turn round slowly. He followed my direction. And then he too witnessed the miraculous propulsion of a carpet across an aisle, through a window, and into a street below. It was now possible for each witness to corroborate the evidence of the other. We ran forward together. And there we caught our culprit quite literally red-handed, his skin chaffed by the coarse weave of the hessian backing of the rugs. His accomplice had already been apprehended by my diligent colleague and at that same moment Saunders arrived with a very sheepish looking fellow in hand-cuffs."

DeVille poured another drink and picked up his half-smoked cigar from the ashtray; he chose not to relight it and put it down again. Looking round he acknowledged our appreciation though he did not require our approval. The fact that we had been willing to listen was enough. And then, as if delivered by some mysterious and hitherto unknown magical force, at that exact

moment in time and no other, a very out of breath Mr Sayed Sadha, arriving beyond the appointed hour for a drinks engagement, flew in from the street, as if through the half-open window – though I cannot be absolutely sure of this – and across the aisle to join DeVille and the gathered assembly. He was welcomed like a long-lost friend. DeVille gave the impression that he was not quite sure what to make of it all.

A Metropolitan Mystery Tour

It all began at the beginning. Well a bit before, actually. I mean, it started before my friend even began to tell the story. Let me explain.

We were seated outside, at a smokers' table, at the *Pig & Whistle*. I had just arrived and was pleased to be here on my old stomping ground once again. I had arranged to meet up with DeVille for a drink. We had not seen each other since the Spring. He had already begun to tell a story to the assembled company and I slipped into my usual role of listener, prompter, and confidante, with accustomed ease.

On this occasion DeVille was, unwittingly, bound for Norfolk, a county only slightly better known to him than its much quieter neighbour Suffolk. He had once before been to Norfolk, to the City of Norwich to be precise, to visit the cathedral with his father on a mystery tour. At that time he was only a child and had been off school with persistent tonsillitis. He remembered very little of the excursion. He did, however, remember walking along a narrow winding street that was called *The Shambles*. They had found a tea shop and he had had a slice of his favourite Victoria sponge cake. Otherwise he had no recollection of the place at all. Of Suffolk he knew almost nothing. He had never been to Ipswich or Lowestoft and only once taken the ferry from Harwich to the Hook of Holland. That was on some sort of smuggling-related business.

DeVille began:

"Let me attempt to explain some of the founding elements of this adventure, or misadventure, as it may be. It all began with the discovery of a burnt-out car used in a bank robbery. Very little was identifiable from the remains of this vehicle. However, there was a single identification mark, just discernible, on the front passenger-side door. This enabled forensics to gather critical information. A search of the relevant databases led to the identification of a vehicle and that vehicle's previous owner, a Mr Farrell, who was registered as living in Norfolk."

We halted for a few minutes as DeVille called for another bottle of Prosecco. DeVille continued to pour generously and all were held in the rambling circle of his story. There was Raul, originally from South West Africa (Namibia), two trainee lady magistrates, a handful of his regulars, and myself. Occasionally the barman, in less busy moments, would lean into the story to catch the gist. It was early in the evening and prospects were good for another couple of hours at least.

After a little while DeVille continued, explaining how matters unfolded. It was like this:

The night before they departed for the rural expanse of Norfolk, DeVille called Mr Farrell at his home. He explained that they wished to come and see him about the car he had sold some two months earlier. He explained that they wanted to know more about who he had sold the vehicle to. Mr Farrell said he would be happy to answer their questions and was sure he had some paperwork somewhere that would be helpful. DeVille rang off, satisfied he had established a lead worth pursuing.

The pool car was signed out by Saunders and together he and DeVille set off to find the M11/A11. I asked if they had a map to help them and was assured they had, only neither was able to read it. This I found somewhat surprising, and said so, but I was assured nothing in their police training had required them to be experts in orienteering. Nonetheless they managed to discover the A11 and headed in the general direction of North-East towards Norwich. It was not very long before they found themselves pulled over into a lay-by, on the aforementioned A11, still some considerable distance from their intended destination. I asked why they had stopped?

DeVille responded with a raised eyebrow and withdrew another small cigar from his rapidly diminishing packet of *Tom Thumbs*. I offered him a light. Then he continued:

"Well, the exhaust-box had fallen off our immaculately maintained vehicle and the sound of our *Metropolitan Maserati* had, as luck would have it, been detected by the local traffic police. A motorcycle patrolman waved us down."

DeVille wound down the driver's window as the officer approached from in front of them, removing his helmet as he did so and revealing a fine red moustache that twirled at each extent like that of an old-fashioned Wing Commander of the R.A.F. Saunders reached over and showed the officer his warrant card. The patrol officer looked at the ID with curiosity and puzzlement.

'Good morning Gentlemen, representing the Met at *Le Mans* then, are we?'

'No, not exactly,' DeVille replied, admiring the line of enquiry.'

'Well, we can't have you going around making all that noise now can we? Never make a collar advertising your presence so plainly. But don't worry, I'm sure we will be able to help, despite our limited rural resources. It's not often we see important detectives like yourselves up from London, not in these parts. I'll get a truck to tow you to the nearest *KwikFit*.'

After what seemed a long and embarrassing wait of some twenty minutes or so, the mighty Met were duly towed to the garage and there they sat watching and waiting as a new exhaust was fitted. Then at last they were in their way once again.

Eventually the road they were on grew increasingly obscure and muddy. As soon as they had turned off the main road they found themselves in a maze of country lanes. Occasionally high hedges would give way to vistas of fenland, dark stretches of almost black earth. As they stopped at a crossroads to consult the map, having seemingly forgotten that neither was at all proficient, DeVille noticed a field full of orange balls – pumpkins in fact – arranged in neat rows. Soon these would be harvested for the strange merriment of Halloween. He thought of the time he was a boy throwing bangers at passing cars or dancing around the burning Guy on the bonfire, followed by potatoes baked in the ashes. They moved on. Narrow lanes turned to single-track roads with passing places, then no passing places, and eventually onto a long track, something like a causeway, across the now un-hedged open fields. Tractor-rutted and cinder-filled, the track filed straight towards a distant single-storey red-brick farmhouse.

DeVille continued:

"When we eventually arrived at the gate to the property – a wide metal gate with chicken-wire attached to it – I asked Saunders to get out and open it. He was not really dressed for the occasion and his beautiful shiny brogues were soon caked in mud and worse. Just as he proceeded to open the gate a flurry of ducks and chickens appeared, as if out of nowhere but actually from around the corner of the house and beyond the coal-bunker, and duly hurled themselves through the open gate and out into the fields beyond. I drove on through the now wide-open gate. Saunders closed it. Only a few stragglers remained in the fold."

DeVille paused, then he sipped at his drink and lit another cigar. We all looked at each other and then back at DeVille, hoping he would continue. It was a good bet. But not before another couple of bottles of Prosecco arrived at our table, courtesy of the part-time member of the audience and permanent barman. DeVille continued:

"I knocked on the door of the house. It was opened by a young lad of perhaps about eighteen or nineteen, judging by the weak stubble on his chin. I introduced myself and showed him my ID."

'May I speak to Mr Farrell please?'

'Mr Farrell is in the parlour', he answered.

'I see. Can I speak to him please?'

He looked at me a moment and then, rather carefully, answered once more:

'No, I'm afraid not, he is in the parlour.'

'Yes, so you said. I spoke to him last night on the telephone and arranged to come and see him.'

'Oh I see. Well you must have been the last person to speak to him then.'

'Why's that?' I asked, beginning to suspect something was not quite right.'

'Like I said, 'cause he is in the parlour. Do you want to speak to *young* Mr Farrell? He's just finished the milking. Here he comes now.'

Young Mr Farrell was not a day over seventy and wore bright green wellington boots, with an orange bale-string around his ample middle, holding up his sagging trousers.

'Funny that,' he said, 'what with you being the last one to speak to him an' all.'

'Yes, so I gather.'

'Oh I'm sure it wasn't your fault. He was on his last legs already. Had been for some time really. We found him in bed this morning quite dead. We laid him out in the parlour. Folks will be wanting to come and pay their respects, you know.'

And now indeed I did gather. Nevertheless I proceeded to

establish that the vehicle in question – the one that, a very long time ago now in this story – had been used in the armed robbery of a bank, had been sold to a couple of blokes from Birmingham. Paid cash. Still had it in the tea caddy on the mantelpiece, if I wanted to see it. I asked about paperwork, in the vain hope there might be some. Even older Mr Farrell had said something about paperwork.

'We don't have no paperwork as such but I do have this picture.'

Young Mr Farrell took out his i-Phone from his inside jacket pocket and proceeded to slide through a series of photographs. He stopped when he reached one of a blue Range Rover.

'Always wanted one of these myself,' he said, 'I took a picture of this when them blokes came to collect the old car they bought from us. Couldn't understand why they wanted it really.'

Not only was it a picture of a Range Rover but it clearly showed its number plate. This was definitely a breakthrough."

But this was not the end of the story, as DeVille went on to explain:

"We'd done what we came to do and, short of actually entering the parlour to pay our respects, felt we had completed this part of the job as best we could. So we set off back to town driving, this time, as smoothly and as silently as an undetected eagle hunting its prey. Unfortunately we had not realised the rarity of petrol stations deep in the darkest countryside and so we managed to run out of petrol. So there we were, on the side of the road in the middle of nowhere, with daylight rapidly fading, with no petrol, rapidly going nowhere. Those days the Met didn't run to radios in all its unmarked vehicles, certainly not the one we'd signed out, and of course this was in the days before we all had our own mobile phones – yes, I'm old enough to remember the last century! Anyway, I got out to see if we had a petrol-can in the boot of the *Maserati* when a police patrol car drew up behind us.

Saunders wound down the window and looked in the driver's wing-mirror. An officer sporting a fine red moustache stepped out of the patrol vehicle and approached us with a broad smile. He waived aside Saunders' ID card.

'Good afternoon, gentlemen. I see the Met's on a stakeout now is it? Hope I'm not getting in the way at all?'

'No not at all, glad to see you in fact,' DeVille replied and proceeded to explain.

'Not a problem, I'm sure we will be able to help, despite our rather limited rural resources. I'll get a truck to tow you to the depot. You can fill her up there,' he explained."

After what seemed a long and embarrassing wait of some twenty minutes or so, the mighty Met were duly towed into the depot and there they sat as the thirsty car's petrol tank was filled. Then once again they were in their way.

But the story was still not over, not quite, not yet. Some two weeks later, after this unlikely excursion into the rural habitat, a letter arrived on DeVille's desk. There was a note attached from his Super' and it stated quite plainly and simply: "*All Yours*". It was a bill from the Fakenham Police Depot for 44 litres of Super unleaded petrol.

On the Other Side of the Street

Some people are said to be *born on the wrong side of the tracks*. This indicates their lesser standing amongst the social classes. Others are born with *a silver spoon in their mouth*, indicating an inherited privilege that confers certain rights and expectations. And others, regardless of where they were born, simply happen to be on the wrong side of the street when it all goes pear-shaped. On this particular day such was the case for DeVille.

The day had begun as an ordinary day. Most days begin in that way – unless you are interrupted from slumber by an irritating and insistent call on the telephone. This day had begun with a cup of sweet coffee on the way to the station. Breakfast could wait; coffee could not.

A call was taken. *The Italian* had been spotted. He was visiting his girlfriend. He had been there all night. Catch him early in the morning. That was the plan. Before he was awake or alert or even suspecting anyone was on to him. He was thought to be armed but that was no matter. He was wanted for drug dealing – he was wanted by Interpol. There was a job to be done and DeVille was willing to do it. Unfortunately, that morning, he was on the wrong side of the street.

His partner, Saunders, R., ex-Horse Guards, and unlikely fan of *Heavy Metal*, was nowhere to be seen. Rather he had been seen, but was no longer to be seen. I'm afraid his shoes were to blame. Saunders, R., had the most highly polished brogues known to the force. According to his army training, it was the shoe, the whole shoe, and nothing but the shoe that was dearly loved with spit and polish every day, without fail. Laces were removed beforehand and replaced carefully afterwards. The exact procedural detail of this ritual, and the precise recipe of the finest polish employed, were a secret known only to him. Needless to say the whole process bore more than a hint of OCDC about it.

Unfortunately, the law of unintended consequences has an alarming if predictable habit of intervening at the most unexpected moments. This was precisely the case this morning. Let us turn the clock back only a few minutes and listen in on DeVille and Saunders as they sit, wrapped up in a padded ski jacket and greatcoat respectively, in their cold and unmarked police car, staking out the house of the girlfriend of the suspect:

"You say he's likely to be armed then?" enquired DeVille, shifting in his seat and trying to get comfortable.

Saunders did not answer. His white earphones were firmly planted in his skull and he was listening intently to Black Sabbath.

DeVille tried again, this time deftly removing the near-side earphone before repeating his question.

"Oh yes. Most probably". replied Saunders, "Suspect was seen leaving Smithy's Yard at just after 10 p.m. last night before coming straight here."

"Right. I see. Will have gone there to collect a piece. Ops might have alerted us beforehand," DeVille mused dryly.

"Not necessary. The ARU are on their way. We're just supposed to watch," replied Saunders.

It was as they were watching that the suspect, Bergoni, came out of the front door and down the Portland steps to the Kensington pavement. Then everything seemed to happen at once, as it does on such occasions:

Despite orders to observe only, DeVille decided the catch was getting away. Not on his watch, he wasn't!

"Come on, let's get the blighter", he called, and pushed open the driver's door half tumbling and half hauling himself out.

Saunders also jumped out, stood upright for an instant, then seemed to kick both legs simultaneously straight up in the air, as if auditioning for the circus in some acrobatic but otherwise unspecified capacity. He slipped and fell flat on his back, completely winded.

Bergoni half-turned briefly as DeVille called after him: "Stop, Police!" Saunders had already stopped. DeVille had not quite started. Bergoni was already running.

Suddenly everything slipped into slow motion as DeVille gathered pace like a Michelin-clad lock-forward racing for the line with no support and utterly on his own. It was at this moment that he began to have doubts, to think upon matters of mortality, to wonder what unfinished business might still be outstanding – perhaps that promise to mow the lawn for his Aunt – and to wonder if he needed to get something in for dinner. All this passed swiftly through his mind as he remembered that the man he was pursuing was most likely armed and undoubtedly willing to shoot.

Unknown to DeVille the Armed Response Unit (ARU) had arrived and were on the other side of the road, running almost alongside, only a few yards behind the main action. From an acute angle of no more than 15 or 20 degrees they suddenly saw what appeared to be a giant human duvet launch itself horizontally towards the fleeing fugitive. Time and space itself seem to stretch for a moment and then, in a vast crumpling of the continuum, the whole weight of matter and anti-matter meets and combines formlessly in a mass of opposing forces. Somewhere beneath the all-embracing eiderdown of the law was Bergoni and gun. Slowly DeVille hauled himself up, then Bergoni, and kicked away the pistol as he applied handcuffs to the captured criminal. Applause rose spontaneously from the *other* side of the street, then cheers and *hip hip hoorays*! DeVille took a bow, and another. Two should suffice, he thought.

The Royal Parks Policeman
or The One That Got Away

The Royal Parks Police (RPP) are similar to the British Transport
Police (BTP) but their jurisdiction covers the heart of London.
Their powers of arrest are restricted to the Royal Parks only and
limited to: common affray, theft of property, or indecent
behaviour.

Today I would be meeting DeVille's former colleague
Robinson, ex RRP. I once had a previous occasion to speak with a
Royal Parks Policeman. It was in my student days, on the
occasion of my leaving the environs of Regents Park carrying a
deck-chair under each arm. I was accompanied by my Theatrical
Director who, fortunately, explained that we were merely
borrowing the deck-chairs for a performance of a one act play by
Bernard Shaw. We had been given permission by the facilities
manager and our word on this matter was, even more fortunately,
accepted. I presume we took the tube back to the East End and
equipped our stage accordingly. I don't recall returning the
deck-chairs but that was the Director's concern at the end of the
day/play, not mine. It was rather a long time ago now. But all this
is by the by, of course.

As an officer in the RPP you had limited scope for
promotion; there was no equivalent to the CID. If you wished
to further your career then it was necessary to do so beyond
the safe and privileged confines of the Royal Parks. You must
leave behind a sheltered existence and take a giant step into the
world beyond, into the cesspits and sewers, the nightclubs and
brothels, of the Great Wen itself, of London, city of the living
and the damned.

One such courageous officer was Robinson (RPP) who, at the
tender age of thirty-five, elected to step into an unknown and
uncertain future. He applied for a transfer to the Met. Robinson
was fortunate, extremely fortunate, though he did not know it at
the time. He was assigned to work under the inimitable tutelage

of DeVille, that master of the unexpected and the curious, that keenest of observers, that most conscientious of mentors.

Robinson was a bit old for school. Nevertheless he had to attend the Detective Training College (DTC) and then do his 'apprenticeship' as a Copper and with CID. He was assigned to DeVille and together they went out one day, both in uniform, on DeVille's usual beat. Together they walked out of Holborn Police Station, along the way, and into Red Lion Square.

I recall interrupting Robinson's account at this point. I had my own personal recollection to offer. Red Lion Square was where, as a boy, I used to go once or twice a year, with my Father, to attend meetings of the Goldfish Society of Great Britain. Of course it is also notorious as a meeting place for all kinds of political agitators and secularists, though I did not know that at the time. But this too is by the by.

Our two Uniforms then proceeded into Prop St., out along Lane Rd., and down to Holborn proper. It was at this point that DeVille appeared to have an idea and, as if plucking a purpose out of nowhere, simply suggested they should stop a few motors. Before Robinson could even nod his assent or query this proposal, DeVille had stepped out into the road, right in front of a white van, holding up his hand as he did so. Robinson gives an eye-witness account:

"I could see that the driver of the van had no intention of stopping. Fortunately, DeVille also realised this and, taking his truncheon from its holster, like a well-practised and well-weathered West End gunslinger, threw the streamlined rod of black *lignum vitae* like a missile, straight through the windscreen, jumping aside at the very last moment! The white van careered on, failing to stop at all. Immediately DeVille hailed a black cab and we both jumped in."

"Follow that van!", cried DeVille.

"You must be jokin' mate!"

"No joke, I assure you," replied DeVille with remarkable composure.

"I've been driving for twenty years now and finally someone – a Copper, no less – asks me to '*follow that van*' – made my day that 'as!"

Robinson continued:

"We hurtled off in hot pursuit and very soon found ourselves near the Mirror building, just down from Holborn Circus. There was the van, smashed into a greengrocer's lorry, and fruit and veg all over the street. The driver's door was wide open and the keys were still in the ignition. The driver had scarpered. Legged it. Done a runner. There was absolutely no sign of him. DeVille popped his head inside the door and quickly found his trusty truncheon. He picked it up from the floor of the van just as the Section Sarge arrived on the scene. Not wishing to appear improperly dressed DeVille discretely re-holstered his truncheon."

"No, don't tell me," said the Sarge, "I'll have your full report on my desk first thing tomorrow morning!"

"But why did DeVille try to stop the van in the first place?" I asked.

"Well, I wondered exactly the same thing ... Do you know what he told me? Well, he said he had no particular reason but, as soon as it failed to stop, he had good reason to believe it was either stolen or transporting stolen property. Sure enough we found crates of expensive champagne in the back of the van. How did we know they were expensive? Well the crates were marked *Harrods*."

When I checked this with DeVille he said that, as far as he remembered, the van belonged to a hire company on the Euston Rd. It had been nicked earlier that same day. He had no recollection of the expensive champagne in the back of the van. However, he did show me a photograph of himself, in full uniform, standing in front of a London cab, with his recently recovered truncheon, highly polished and resplendent, about to be restored to its holster. He was smiling – ruefully, it seemed to me – at the troubling thought of

the one that got away.

The St Pancras Pantomime

DeVille has a new pupil under his wing, Thompson's his name. This trainee detective is pretty wet behind the ears, as he admits, but he will soon learn. And one thing he will certainly learn from DeVille is the canny skill of basing decisions on keen observation. Today they are driving the Q car – the unmarked police car used by CID – and they are parked just outside St. Pancras Station. They have been there for about ten minutes. They have watched buses disgorge and engorge an endless supply of passengers; London cabbies executing skilful U-turns in pursuit of fares; and draymen rolling aluminium barrels off their lorries into vaults hidden beneath the pavement. The combination of these familiar sights, commonplace almost, has a steadily soporific effect. Even the roar of diesel engines and the clanging of beer barrels merely provide a constant and undifferentiated commentary to these daily events.

"Quick Thompson, jump out and grab the keys off that driver!" shouts DeVille.

Woken rudely from his reverie the Trainee leaps into action. Across the road a car has just parked up and the driver is stepping out onto the pavement, car keys in hand. With a cursory glance in each direction the Trainee launches himself like a triple jumper across the road and grabs the keys. The driver seems about to remonstrate but is stopped in his tracks at the sight of the Trainee's ID card, which is held up by way of explanation. A moment or two later DeVille arrives at his side and produces his authority in similar fashion.

"Where did you nick the motor from?" Deville enquires.

"It's not stolen," the driver exclaims!

"Oh yes it is!"

"Oh no it isn't!"

Some passers-by have stopped to see what is happening. They seem to have stumbled into a pantomime. This is confirmed, it seems, when a *Black Maria* pulls up alongside and six uniformed policemen step out to arrest the driver, just as the nearby clock at

St. Pancras Station starts to chime the twelve strikes of midday. Before the chimes had finished the *Black Maria* had swept away in a cloud of diesel fumes. A few moments later a police tow truck arrived to pick up the stolen car. The crowd that had gathered spontaneously, albeit briefly, soon dispersed. Once again the humdrum of routine reasserted itself. DeVille and the Trainee returned to the Q car and headed back to Holborn.

"So why did DeVille tell you to grab the car keys?" I asked Thompson.

In particular, I was interested to learn how he himself was originally introduced to the all-important first principle of the Art of Observation: *Observe*!

"Well, I wondered exactly the same thing, and do you know what he told me? He said it was the number plate, obviously. The letters had been reversed so that ABC 160K had become CAB 160K. Now this was in the days when each letter and number was individually attached to the board plate. But it wasn't anything odd in the order of the letters themselves. No, it was subtler than that. You see the 'shadow' of where the letters had previously been was visible under the new ordering. DeVille's keen eye had spotted this and interpreted it accordingly. The car had been nicked and the number plate changed."

It turned out that the car had been stolen at about four o'clock in the morning that very same day in South Wales. The driver had driven all the way up to London and was looking for a B&B in the Kings Cross area. But he had not accounted for the long arm of the law or, as in this case, the long sight of the law.

When asked later by the Magistrate what he thought of his flying visit to the great Capital, he replied, most forcefully and without a moment's hesitation:

Blimey Bill, I'm not coming up to London again! Your Coppers must have eyes in the back of their heads!

We finished our drinks and I thanked Thompson for his time and for providing his own first-hand account of DeVille at work, practising his well-honed observational methods in the pursuit of London crime.

The Columbo of Kensington

"We were assigned to a murder case. This was an excellent opportunity for my new trainee, Davey, to learn first-hand about the nuances of detective work. But first there were the practicalities and standard procedures. We received what's known as a *Triplicate*. It's a sort of order or directive. It comprises the following actions: an instruction to trace someone, at a given address, and to obtain a statement from them. We were told to trace a certain Columbo at an address in South Kensington. Apparently he would be able to provide a statement regarding the character and habits of the victim."

I smiled at this point and was about to say something – but I just managed to stop myself in time. I had almost taken the bait that DeVille had dangled in front of me[1]. He continued, acknowledging my near-interruption:

"Well I thought this was curious too, I must say. I had visions of meeting Peter Falk himself, the annoyingly persistent American TV detective, his raincoat draped over his arm. Still, if it were him then he would be able to supply a wealth of observational details, I felt sure!"

Davey and DeVille find themselves in the lobby of a grand Edwardian structure, just off Kensington High St. It is a well to do area, as evidenced by the expensive limousines and sports cars arrayed along the street outside. They search the name-plates of the post-boxes and find Columbo's flat is located on the second floor of a rear annexe. They make their way to the back of the main building. Davey bounds up the stairs like an unleashed whippet; DeVille demonstrates a more sober motion, like that of a St Bernard. At the door he gives Davey the privilege of first knock.

A man of about forty or so, dressed in a T-shirt and jeans, answers the door to them. They ask to speak to Mr Columbo.

---

[1] *Well that's not quite how I remember it. You fell for it hook, line and sinker, I seem to recall !* (DeVille).

"Ah you mean Father Columba! Just a minute," he replies and turns round and disappears down an unlit corridor.

Davey and DeVille wait patiently. DeVille observes a faint smell, not overly familiar, but perhaps joss-sticks. After a few moments the man returns, dressed in a flowing habit, with a cord tie around the middle, and wearing open leather sandals.

"Do please come in," he says.

Davey and DeVille follow as he leads them into a small reception room at the end of the corridor.

"How may I help you?" asks Father Columba.

DeVille realises their mistake and begins to apologise for the name confusion but Father Columba waives it aside and smiles reassuringly. He proceeds to explain his position and their surroundings:

They were in the Presbytery of St John the Baptist, an order of Franciscans, where novitiates were trained for the priesthood. Father Columba was both the local Parish Priest and a senior member of the theological teaching staff at the presbytery. The smell that DeVille had detected was incense.

"We believe you knew the deceased?" Davey enquires.

"Yes, I did. You realise, of course, that I cannot reveal anything discovered during the sacrament of confession but I am sure I can give you some helpful information about my late parishioner, your murder victim.

But first may I offer you gentlemen a drink?"

"Just tea for us," said DeVille. Father Columba rang a bell and a novice appeared to take their order.

"Don't mind if I do, I hope?"

"Not at all," replied DeVille.

Father Columba moved across the room and opened the eight-foot wide dresser opposite. It was well-stocked with a large range of drinks. No, it was very well-stocked, virtually over-flowing, with spirits. He poured himself a small dry sherry. Soon tea arrived, together with a plate of chocolate biscuits.

"Where on earth, or in Heaven, did you get all this booze from?" DeVille asked between bites of his biscuit.

"Ah well, you see I have a lot of parishioners in need of forgiveness. Instead of *Hail Marys* I try to find something more effective in bringing my flock back to the straight and narrow. It seems to work. Priests are allowed to drink, you know!"

At that point DeVille reconsidered. He had completed a twelve hour shift and was now officially off duty – timed out, so to speak. "Can I change my mind?" asked DeVille.

"Of course you may!" replied Father Columba.

"I think I'll have a G&T then, if you don't mind."

It was on this occasion that Davey, trainee detective and general lackey thereby, was first introduced to what is known as the *Lifeboat System*. While not included in any official police manual, or not one that I am aware of, it is nonetheless a standard procedure and may be applied whenever deemed necessary. Under this time-honoured system it is the duty of the Junior detective to ensure that his Senior partner is returned without harm, either to himself or to others, to a place of warmth, comfort and safety i.e. home.

Thereafter DeVille used to visit Father Columba every couple of months, though not for confession. Father Columba was a good source of information and much else that related rather tangentially to his professional calling. DeVille learnt an amount of useful *gen* and probably forgot just as much. More than once he required a lift home in a *lifeboat*.

The Earls Court
Hue & Cry

Big Brother is watching. In the United Kingdom, on every corner of every town, on every street in every city, CCTV cameras record our every move: the drunken brawl, the ATM ram-raid, the midnight robbery at an all-night petrol station, the urban fox rummaging through the discards of the day. All these are seen and recorded; all these are sources of evidence to the forces of law and order. But it was not always so.

"We had no CCTV footage to view when I first started on the beat. As far as I recall the first time I ever came across a case where CCTV was important was over in Earls Court. It was a big supermarket somewhere near Olympia, where they used to hold big events like The Ideal Home Exhibition, and American-style Evangelical rallies. But this was probably sometime in the early nineteen-eighties that I'm thinking of."

DeVille and I were seated at a favourite watering-hole. It was a summer's day and the English Monsoon was in full spate. And so was DeVille. He continued unabated:

"I was queuing in the canteen. I had been catching up on paperwork and had just gone to fetch a coffee and a Chelsea bun. Just as I get back to my desk we get a call about pickpockets. Any excuse, I thought, and grabbed my coat, stuffed the bun into the pocket, and made the Sixty-nine bus in seconds flat – our Q car was in dock and not currently roadworthy so we were consigned to Public Transport for the duration. I had two trainees under my care that day as Saunders was off with the flu. Anyway, with coffee in one hand and a bun in the other, my Trainee Davey obliged with the fares – '*and don't forget to keep the tickets so you can reclaim on expenses!*' I said.

On arrival we were shown the security tapes, the better to identify the culprits and to study their particular *modus operandi*. Curiously, they were still operating in the store some twenty minutes after we had first been called. This pair had a nerve, that's for sure. This is what we observed:

A was equipped with a wire basket containing a few items, including some cloths. B had an umbrella with which to 'mark' their target. Once a victim was identified they moved with military speed and precision as they turned like guided missiles honing in on their hapless target, whose handbag was open and whose purse was neatly exposed. The snatcher would then swiftly hand on the 'taking' to his colleague. All this in the proverbial blink of an eye!"

So they spring into action and go to nick 'em. Davey and the other young trainee, Jeffries, go for A who ditches his wire basket and does a runner. Meanwhile DeVille goes for B, the *Umbrella Man*, who jabs him and makes a dash for the exit. DeVille gets up and follows him out. Then he spies him jumping into a taxi which immediately heads off in the direction of Earls Court Rd. DeVille stops an unsuspecting member of the Great British Public (GBP) and commands the startled driver to *"Follow that cab! Don't lose him!"*

Meanwhile the taxi driver quickly realised that the chase was on and his fare was hiding on the floor. He stopped the cab and B threw open the door and made a dash for it.

Moments later DeVille drew up alongside and the cabbie enquired: *"You Old Bill then?"* DeVille nodded. *"Right, hop in. let's get 'im!"* They head off down the Old Brompton Rd. in hot pursuit. Just then B turns and runs back towards them.

"Quick, open the door!" shouts the cabbie as he pulls over to the left and clips B at about 25 mph. He got totally flattened – really took the wind out of his sails!

B was taken by ambulance to Fulham hospital – three teeth were gone and he needed to have his jaw wired.

A couple of weeks later, after he had recovered sufficiently, DeVille arrived to interview him:

"Don't you come near me!" cried B, still traumatised by his brush with the law. It transpired that he had a large number of previous convictions. In the end he got two years for his troubles, and ours," explained DeVille.

"But what of our local London hero?", I wondered.

"Well, needless to say the taxi door was shot – but we got it fixed on the *'hurry up'*," explained DeVille.

"The Judge awarded the cabbie £250 from public funds, which fell due from the Sheriff of London. I advised him to post a copy in his cab in case it was ever useful on the occasion of a red light."

As we left the pub that night with the rain still tipping down in bucket-fulls, DeVille to his taxi and I to catch my train, I noticed the CCTV camera located high in the corner of the room. A green light was flashing to indicate it was working. I wondered if it had recorded anything of what we had said. Was it merely watching or had it perhaps been listening too?

A Crime-Fighter's Career

It has been suggested that the stories in this series, describing DeVille's curious exploits and notorious anecdotes, should be presented chronologically. In this way we would see the development of his career and his character and one tale would naturally lead to another, in sequential order. This is a plausible, if not actually possible, approach: plausible as it has a degree of logic to it; impossible because DeVille neither recalls nor relates things chronologically. Instead we are privy to occasional insights into his career, as they arise whilst he is guiding and leading/misleading us down a twisting track of his own devising. We merely glimpse snippets of his *Policeman's Progress*. However, in this piece I shall gather up some of those snippets and try to stitch them together into a sort of patch-work quilt. To what extent the resulting work will be accurate remains to be seen. However, I shall endeavour to remain as faithful as possible to DeVille's own account without recourse either to public records, professional certificates, or other types of evidence as may be admissible in a Court of Law. This I believe to be an approach that is in harmony with the original. Whether DeVille is an honest pedlar of tales, or a rogue narrator of fantasy, I must leave you to judge for yourself.

But enough of this preamble. What of DeVille? What is he doing out of uniform with his tie undone and his jacket off? Let me tell you what he has told me:[2]

"When in uniform a policeman was not allowed to claim plain clothes allowance (the princely sum of £10 per month). Furthermore he was only allowed to do ninety days per year as a temporary plain clothes officer."

DeVille himself recalls that he was already well known in the Force as an efficient *nabber of crooks*. This probably gave him a head start, or a step-up, when it came to consideration as a candidate for promotion. His opportunity arose as follows:

---

[2] Taken from notes to a late night phone call.

"I seemed to have been noticed around about the time of the First Hatton Garden Vault robbery in 1972-3. I was appointed as uniformed officer set to guard the front door. I had been selected by C.I. Walker who then recommended me to work as Inspector – that was in about September/October. At that time we were allowed to 'act up' as non-uniform for a period of up to ninety days a year only, as I think I mentioned before. Anyway, this gave us *Bobbies* the chance of experiencing detective work *and* helped to build rapport with C.I.D. As it happened I then worked another ninety days, back-to-back. So I had already been doing a fair amount of continuous plain clothes work when I took my probation exams. This was very unusual. Basically I was fast-tracked because I was jolly good at the job! But then again, I had been taught by some excellent people – ex-Services, good Detectives, people who believed in what they were doing, in the importance of how they did it, and who wanted to pass on that whole ethos, as well as the relevant skills and techniques. I was very lucky."

All this is tantalising. What else do we wish to know about DeVille's career and how can we find out? Perhaps I should prepare a set of written questions for him? Let's see:

Q.1. When and where did you first enter the Police Force?

Q.2. Please state your reasons for wishing to join the Police Service?

Q.3. What ranks have you held and when did you attain each of these?

Q.4. Are you now or have you ever been a member of either a) the Communist Party, or b) the Church of England?

Q.5. Have you received any commendations or medals? Please describe these in full.

Q.6. When did you retire from the Force? Why?

Q.7. Did you take up any other employment after retirement from the Force?

Q.8. Have you ever signed the Official Secrets Act? (No, don't answer that, it might compromise you).

But then again that seems too obvious, too dry, too predictable an approach. What I am looking to capture and recreate is the experience that is DeVille himself in full narrative flight – his career details are purely incidental to this.

At this point I decided to send a draft copy of this piece to DeVille. He duly obliged by responding with some files that I could not read without downloading a ZIP programme – which I am now in the process of doing. Suffice to say I will soon have gleaned more information but, for the moment, it remains just out of reach!

{ sometime later … }

I have now managed to read DeVille's attachments. Apparently he received an award for knocking someone out. We begin *in medias res.*

"I was flagged down on my way home at about eleven one night. The victim was stabbed in the neck with the stem of a gin glass outside a pub in Chelsea. By midnight he was still bleeding profusely. I applied a tourniquet. Just then I saw a police van coming the other way. I hailed it and saw it was Taff from Melsham. Lucky for me. He turned round his van and turned on the flashing blue light. I followed in my car but my bleeding passenger just wouldn't stop shouting and screaming. So I stopped the car, turned round and punched him in the face, just to shut him up. Off we went again with the flashing blue light and bell – it was in the days before we had sirens – and made for the nearest A&E. He had emergency surgery and that saved his life[3]."

But that is not the end of the story …

"Anyway, about three years later he's claiming compensation from the C.I.C.B. (Criminal Injuries Compensation Board)[4] – for being stabbed – not because I knocked him out! My name comes up in the Board's review when the A&E surgeon's letter, commending my life-saving action, comes to light. It had been filed away by the investigating officer among other important papers and case notes. As a result of its rediscovery I was

---

[3] Both the application and *removal* of the tourniquet also played a part in this favourable outcome.

[4] The purpose of which is to provide assistance to victims of violent crime. Specific tariffs are defined per injury. A victim must agree to give evidence. However a claim cannot be made if said victim has a violent criminal record.

recommended for a *Humane Society* award. Unfortunately there was no pension with it, just a certificate on vellum.

It turned out later that the chap I saved, Geoff Little his name was, was a costermonger down at the Portobello Street market, a well-known *fruit & veg* man. Anyway, sometime later – not long after – I got talking to a local councillor. Jennifer Jones was well known and well respected in the local community. I told her that I'd never had any compensation for my ruined shirt – the one I'd used to try and stop the bleeding – and the mess all over the back seat of my car had to be cleaned up at great personal expense. I only realised later that she had taken me seriously. This was when she arranged for the Mayor of Kensington & Chelsea to award me a certificate and the whole family were invited to come and see the presentation. So there we all are, pomp and ceremony, me with a suit and tie and shoes as shiny as any Saunders ever polished. *Blow me down*, also there is Geoff Little, Portobello costermonger!

The Mayor, in all his fine regalia, presents me with a fifty pound note, drawn from the civic fund and in his official gift – it's for a new shirt, he says. Meanwhile, standing right behind me and breathing down my neck, is the Chief of Police. I hear him whisper in an unmistakable and audible fashion: 'You give that back, DeVille.' For once I did as I was told, though I must admit reluctantly! And then the splendid Mayor presents me with a gallon drum of the finest Scottish Malt Whisky on behalf of Geoff Little, the man whose life I'd saved. Well, I wasn't going to refuse that now, was I? Interestingly I did not hear the voice of Jiminy Cricket over my shoulder this time. Instead there was an acquiescent silence of approval. And then – there's more – the Mayor called me aside after the presentation and said: "Have a word with Jennifer before you go, won't you? So I did. She handed me the fifty pound note and said not to mention it.

A few weeks later I was attending a dinner at the Civil Service Club in Whitehall, just down the road from Trafalgar Square. I'd been to a Lodge Meeting where a charitable fund-raising event was in the planning. I was chatting to a couple of the ladies who were waitressing for the evening. Apparently one of them worked down at Portobello Market.

'How well do you know it?' she asks me.

'Pretty well', I said.

'Do you know Geoff Little on the fruit&veg stall? He's my cousin. You're not the copper who saved his life, are you?'

'Well yes, I suppose I am.'

The next thing was the biggest brandy glass you ever did see arrives at my table – and its full of excellent cognac!

And after that I never wanted for fresh fruit or veg! Sacks of potatoes, and boxes of melons and crates of bananas used to arrive at the station for me. I became known as the *Greengrocer* and would offer my goods for sale at knockdown prices to my colleagues:

Luverly strawbreeze! Get yer bananas 'ere! Pound-a-pound!

Human Nature

"People haven't changed. I mean, the way they behave hasn't changed. Of course the cars they drive, the fact that everyone has a car, the speed they drive at and the pace of life– all these have changed. But underneath all that, human nature is essentially the same. You've got the same types of mentalities. People like to belong to groups and gangs, they often have strong family ties – blood is still thicker than water – and they don't like to put themselves out any more than they have to. At the same time, you can't forget that there are always a few exceptions to the rule, in any age and in any place. I've always found that to be so."

DeVille was expounding his view of human nature in general and the criminal mind in particular. In fact he was expounding on the human condition itself: the context and environment within which individuals and society exist. He was no political

theorist, but obviously inclined, by upbringing and his own moral temperament, towards ideas of individual responsibility. On the other hand he was also naturally conservative. He liked order and tradition but he also liked to buck the trend. He had no time for incompetent and arbitrary authority.

When I first met DeVille he was driving courtesy buses for a well-known chain of hotels. I was staying at one of these hotels while working up in London during the week.

"So tell me, what did you do before driving the shuttle bus?"

"I used to do murders," he said.

"Ah ... in what way exactly?"

"I was in the Met," he said, "and for a while I was in the Murder Squad."

"Oh ! So you were a detective then?"

"Yes. In the Met First. Then Scotland Yard too, but that was a bit later."

It was some time after we had reached the hotel before I finally made it to reception and collected my key. I didn't realise at the time that this initial exposure to DeVille's tales of the unexpected (and quite often preposterous) was just the tip of the iceberg. I was to participate in many more story-telling episodes over the next few years: when we met for a drink at the pub; at a family garden party with food and drink to share. Any occasion was a good excuse for Deville, and for me too.

It is curious how you make friends in later life. Too often people are just colleagues. Of course family commitments mean you haven't got the time to be out and about after work or in the evenings. But then an odd thing happens. The nest is empty and the children are gone. You have time on your hands and a list of projects ranging from railway set construction in the attic to writing a blockbuster thriller novel for the airport terminal. But every time you start one project another interrupts and many are left unfinished as a result. Maintaining old friendships becomes embarrassingly haphazard over the years. Gradually you discover that new friendships, without baggage, are just the thing. You find you have things in common. Then, before you know where you are, you find yourself committing, promising, and even writing someone else's story because it is far more interesting than your own.

DeVille began:

"I was just a young copper then. My beat took in the area around Holborn and included Hatton Gardens. That's where that big robbery happened not so long ago. You remember?"

I did.

"Well, it was freezing that night. I was new on the force, not long out of school, so to speak. Of course most of our learning as young coppers was done on the beat in them days, though we did do a day-release over at Wandsworth College.

Let me tell you about that time, out on the beat, learning the ropes, as it were. And like I said, or should have said if I didn't before, it was really cold– brass monkey weather – and you had to keep moving just to keep from freezing. Well at about half-past eleven that night I'm a bit surprised to see a patrol car pull up outside the Post Office. I thought maybe they were checking up on me, see if I was alright, or at least not skiving off. One of the officers hops out and soon ducks down an alley off the Holborn Road, leaving his partner at the wheel. I shifted into a darkened doorway on the opposite side of the street and observed. Like I was trained to do. So I did. A few minutes later the first bloke comes back out of the alley and gets back into the patrol car. And off they go. So I decided to cross the road and go and investigate. The alley was a dead-end. At the far end was the back of the old Red Lion pub; not sure if that's still there now, but anyway, it was then."

DeVille coughed and scratched his arm. He picked up his glass of wine and took a sip, savouring the moment. And then, pause for effect complete, he continued:

"So, suspicions aroused, I watched out for this same thing the next night at about the same time. Sure enough the same thing happened. By the third night I had already investigated the spot by eleven o'clock. When the patrol car turned up a bit later, and the copper went into the alley as usual, he was disappointed to find that his usual toddy was missing. The bottle of stout left out under a milk-crate was there alright but it was empty. Now I should say at this point that I am not myself a drinker of ale – never have been. No, I had merely disposed of the incriminating evidence by tipping it down the drain. You see it was all part of what you had to learn as a rookie – it wasn't a bribe as such, more an oiling of the wheels. It encouraged the police to keep an eye on the pub, out the back. I suppose some would say it was corrupt but I don't really see it that way. Still, I knew enough not to say anything to anyone, especially not the Sarge."

I can't be sure I'm getting all the details of the story right, but does it matter? It's surely more important to remain truthful to the spirit of the Deville experience rather than just the letter.

"I don't think you've heard this story before. Do you know what a 'Door Knocker' is?"

Well, I thought I did, but apparently not. (Nothing at all to do with the face of Jacob Marley and the fright it gave poor Scrooge apparently) A 'Door Knocker' is in fact a speculative caller searching for antiques and curios that a householder might agree to sell to raise a bit of cash, or have simply grown tired of and wish to move it on. Of course, this practice was open to abuse[5].

"No, well, one day about midday we got a call from a contact in the antiques trade. A bloke had tried to interest him in a French clock for one hundred and fifty quid. Only trouble was the antiques dealer reckoned it was worth about eight thousand quid!

Anyway, this bloke had a lot of interesting objects in the back of his van, especially the rather fine clock. Looked suspicious to me so we invited him back to the station to check all his goods and to compare them with our own register of stolen property. It turned out that he also had a carefully rolled-up oil-painting that he said he'd bought for a few quid up in Edinburgh, or so he said. We had a *shufti* and it looked like it might be worth a lot more than that. So I decided to show it to a chap I knew – friend of a friend – who worked on Portobello market. Anyway, to cut a long story short, he reckoned it was probably worth about ten grand! So I contacted our lads north of the border and asked them to find out if it had been a genuine sale.

I asked the Desk Sergeant to store it away safely under lock and key for the night; tomorrow we'd make a few calls to see if any of the major galleries were missing a grand master!"

DeVille coughed again and drew another cigar from his packet of five. I picked up the lighter and lit it for him.

"Now here's a bit of background you need to know," said DeVille in an almost conspiratorial tone, "The three Ps."

"The Three Ps?" I echoed.

"Yes, the Three Ps: Property, Prisoners, and Prostitutes."

"What about them?" I asked, puzzled.

"Well, those are the three things that every copper is taught to handle very carefully, for different reasons of course, but carefully nonetheless."

---

[5] Or as DeVille put it, after reading my imperfect account: *"Door Knockers emanated from Brighton, probably because of The Lanes, an area known for its small antique shops. Doorknockers roamed the country door-knocking in an effort to find antiquities. They chose the houses very carefully. A house with grey net curtains, lack of outside decoration, normally indicates someone elderly. A prime target/victim. This is not to say all Door Knockers were criminals, but among their ranks, there were many who would take the opportunity, at the drop of a knock."*

I was beginning to see where this might be going but could not be sure. DeVille continued:

"The next day I arrive at the station at about nine-thirty. We'd been working late on an *opo* in the East End so I wasn't as bright and early as usual. The shifts had changed and there were a new set on duty in the office. I asked the daytime Desk Sergeant if I could have the painting, so I could do some phoning-round about it."

"Yes, of course," he said, "I've got it right here."

"What do you mean, it's supposed to be under lock and key."

"Yes, it is. It's here in the safe."

"What do you mean, it's in the safe. It can't fit in there, it's a painting and it's about sixteen inches by twenty-four – the safe is only twelve-by-twelve! It should be in the property store."

"No, it's definitely here," he replied.

"He then proceeded to unlock the safe and withdraw a neatly folded oil painting. It was halved and halved again and halved once more. It had been folded up like an ordnance survey map. You could have played noughts and crosses on it. He proceeded to open it out to reveal the full picture once more, complete with creases. A ten grand painting!"

"Criminal damage!" I exclaimed.

"Exactly. For once I was completely lost for words."

"I find that hard to believe," I said.

"Well, I'm full of surprises!

"Indeed. Do carry on."

"Well, I made some enquiries with colleagues up in Edinburgh. Apparently the lady had originally bought it, way back in the early 1970's, for two shillings and sixpence (about 12 new pence) at a jumble sale in Morningside. She had been keen to know if she had sold it for a good price at fifty pounds. I telephoned her and was able to provide reassurance that it wasn't worth any more than that – though I omitted to add '*in its current state*'!

Anyway, about an hour later our van-man comes in to collect his fifty-quid purchase. I tell him we won't be pressing any charges on this occasion and that he can take the long clock an' all as none of it is on the *official* list of stolen property. Then I handed him the painting. For a moment he stared, mouth wide open, his face was an absolute picture – not creased exactly, more of a shocked grimaced, I'd say!"

What's in a Name?

————————

"I get a call from Constable Jimmy Jones," explains DeVille, "and he tells me he's doing a burglary."

"What?" says I, "a burglary?"

"Yes," says he, "a burglary."

"Well," says I, "a funny kind of copper you are!"

"No Sarge, no. I'm *investigating* a burglary!" says Jimmy.

"Oh I see!" says I.

Anyways, Jimmy sounds as if he might be choking on the other end of the phone. Then I realise it's him laughing, or rather him trying not to laugh.

"What's up Jimmy? What's so funny?" I ask.

"Well," says Jimmy, "I just had a word with this chap who said he'd seen some blokes skulking off with a few pallets from the DIY warehouse down Purley Way."

"Ok, so I'm not laughing yet," says I.

"No? Well (*interruption … for cough … ing fit*) that's because I haven't got to the best part yet."

"Well hurry up then. I want to hear the joke before you croak!"

"I've just interviewed a … lorry … driver – *ha ha ha … gasp*!"

"Well it *still* ain't funny!" I says.

"Yes, I know. But his name … his name – *ha ha ha, ha ha ha*!"

"What about his name?" I ask.

"Lawrence."

"Lawrence. Yes, so? Still not funny, I'm afraid," I tell him.

"Mr Driver!"

At this point Jimmy completely collapses into a wailing and laughing heap, totally unable to control himself for a moment longer."

Then it starts to dawn on DeVille: The sun begins to rise – the realisation, the understanding, the revelation!

"Lawrence – Larry, Lawrie, Lorry

… Driver

… The *lorry driver*!"

DeVille sniggers, trying to supress an involuntary reflex to laugh.

"You're taking the pro*verb*ial," I says.

But then there is another involuntary reflex and DeVille's willpower collapses around him like a discarded raincape. He too collapses like a blancmange into a heap of uncontrollable laughter!

"Of course, you came across many odd names in a lifetime of policing," DeVille explains, "and this was just one of them."

"Yes, I know what you mean," I said, "Like Mr De'ath the Undertaker."

"Exactly!" said DeVille, "case in point. Then there was Gottfried Lost, the adventurer and explorer, TV personality. Had to be rescued from the ice and snow in Hartlepool, on his way up to the Arctic."

"Really?" I asked.

"No, not really. It wasn't Hartlepool. It was Coldstream."

"Ha! And what about The Reverend Lewis Cipher?"

And then the phone rang. It was Jimmy. Constable Jimmy Jones.

"I'm doing a burglary," he said.

A Twist of Fate

DeVille realised that the very beginning of his story gave something away regarding the nature of its conclusion. The clue was, of course, in the title. But what was not immediately evident was that this was to be a darker and more sombre story than most, concerning serious crimes against the person. It is not for the faint-hearted, nor those of a nervous disposition. However, I would ask you to bear with me while I try to do his story justice.

On this particular evening we were, as often, gathered together informally at the *Pig & Whistle*, not far from Waterloo Station. We were a selected audience, some invited, and others included, but all welcome to the feast. The drink began to flow freely and DeVille became even more convivial than usual. He had already waxed lyrical on the different sounds and effects of various church and chapel organs and harmoniums. This was a subject he was expert on since childhood. Whilst his father, a peripatetic organist, played the hymn tunes and the congregation sang loudly and enthusiastically, but always lagging behind, the boy DeVille would be engaged in supplying sufficient pressure of air to the acoustic instrument by way of whatever bellows, pedals, or pumps were provided for that particular purpose.

He claimed this resulted in the prodigious muscles that later enabled him to become U.K. Police Force lightweight boxing champion. We took him at his word, though I wondered about his onetime membership of the 'lightweight' division. But discretion is always the better part of valour and I let him continue uninterrupted:

"We knew who it was but we couldn't prove it! How many times have I said that? We were called to a flat down near Shadwell."

"Not your usual patch then?" I enquired.

"No, that's right. They must have been short-staffed at the time. We used to do a bit of cover now and again. Anyway, we were called to a flat down near Shadwell. It was about eleven o'clock one night. A WPC was there ahead of us comforting an old lady. She had been beaten and raped by an intruder. She was unable to answer any questions at that point and the WPC went with her in the ambulance to hospital. We questioned her just before she left the hospital a few days later and she was able to give us a partial description of her attacker. From this we identified a likely suspect, someone who lived in the same block of flats and had a record but no alibi."

DeVille stopped for a moment, as if reflecting, and I thought I saw a moment's sign of rage flicker across his face. I realised then that this was a story that had affected DeVille more than he might be willing to admit. It was as if he needed to release his own anger and disgust, all the emotions that he had previously had to hold back in the course of his work, in performing his duty. Only now, in the recounting of his experiences to another captive audience, was he able to find some kind of remission. And this was curious as these were not his own sins that he confessed but those of others, of the evil and the wicked, whom he had found, without doubt, to exist in the world.

"To cut a long story short," said DeVille,

(something I would never accuse him of)

"As I say, we identified a suspect but anything except circumstantial evidence was scarce. We asked the old lady to attend an identification parade. Of course we had to be scrupulous not to direct or lead her in any way. I must say I admired her courage. I mean, it can't have been an easy thing to do, can it? Anyway, we had half a dozen dodgy looking characters lined up, including the suspect, of course, and the off-duty police dog-handler, just for good measure. When asked if she could identify anyone she said:

'*I don't see him*'.

Technically this meant *no identification*, and so we had to let our suspect go. We were gutted.

It was about a month or so later that we got our breakthrough. There was another violent assault, of a similar nature, on another elderly lady, but this time her attacker was disturbed. That evening the lady's upstairs neighbour was expecting a gentleman visitor and, as he arrived, he heard a crashing noise and screaming. A figure dashed out of the apartment below and fled down the staircase. He gave chase but failed to catch the man, who escaped by climbing over a high gate topped with barbed wire. In so doing, he did himself an injury, as a patch of freshly spilled blood, discovered by the SOCOs, duly testified. In addition, he dropped a set of keys as he was climbing over the gate. His pursuer picked these up and handed them over to us, along with a detailed witness statement. Unfortunately he had not seen the face of the man he had chased."

"So what was your next move?" I asked.

"Simple. I looked at the keys and saw id numbers on two of them. I called the on-duty locksmith (always useful to have one readily available in my line of work, you know). Anyway, he came over and duly identified the keys for me. And you know what?

"No, what?" I said.

"Well, let me tell you. Those numbers revealed that the keys were standard issue for the local borough council. So next morning I called the Estates Office and spoke to the manager. He was soon able to tell me the address to which the keys belonged. It was an apartment in the very same block of flats where the victim of the first attack lived.

Meanwhile the local general hospital reported that a man had attended A&E that evening, a man who had seriously damaged his undercarriage and possibly his prospects too.

This time the CPS decided we had enough evidence to warrant a prosecution. We'd caught the b...d!"

Now we are transported to the Old Bailey. It is the day of the trial and DeVille is there to give evidence. With him today is his young trainee Jeffries (no relation to the judge). Jeffries' grandmother, Mrs Eliza Jeffries, has always wanted to visit the Old Baily and today she has obtained a seat in the public gallery, along with her friend and neighbour Mrs Meredith Hobbes. They are equally fascinated and appalled as the case is outlined in court during the preliminaries. After an hour, at eleven a.m. precisely, the judge adjudicates that a break for coffee is due, if not by law then by the norms of civilised society, at the very least. These he assesses to be in harmony with his own thoughts and wishes: two sugars and a stem ginger biscuit in chambers will do very nicely just now!

As the court is returning and settling down after this short interval, the defending barrister, a Mr Hardcastle Q.C. of Lincolns Inn, I believe, notices the arresting officer DeVille and another younger policeman. They are talking to two elderly ladies seated in the gallery. With the razor-sharp mind of a sun-blazed lizard he puts two and two together in lightning-quick fashion. And he makes five. The two ladies are not in fact the victims of the crimes, come to give evidence against his client but, thinking that they are, he determines the best advice for his client. He advises him to plead guilty to the lesser charge of indecent assault in both instances.

Now this was good advice. I mean it *was* good advice. But given a recent change in the law regarding the sentencing policy for this charge, it was *no longer* good advice. It was in fact rather bad advice, mistaken if you will, as both he and his client, and we, would shortly discover.

Instead of a maximum prison term of two years for the charge of indecent assault, the maximum had now been raised to ten years. In theory the defendant could have received a maximum of twenty years in prison i.e. two lots of full-term sentences of ten years. However, the esteemed judge presiding at the Old Bailey, that day in Court Number Three, deemed that two five-year consecutive sentences were justified in this particular case. So the defendant went down for a total of ten years. He was totally shocked and swiftly led from the court screaming and cursing, as you can imagine!

But that is not quite the end of this story. I will let DeVille tell us in his own words:

"Yes, thank you. Very kind."

"All yours!"

"Right. Well, it was late in the afternoon when we finished at the Old Bailey that day and retired across the road to the *Magpie & Stump*."

"Real name?" I asked.

"Yes, real name."

"Just checking."

"The *Magpie and Stump*. Hadn't been there in a long time! Anyway, Jeffries was about to get the drinks in, though he didn't know it yet. Just then Mr Harcourt appeared, unwigged, disrobed and ruddy-cheeked, in the lawyer's equivalent of *mufti*. He hailed us and strode over to where we were sitting."

"Can I buy you chaps a drink?" he enquired.

"We're off duty, aren't we Jeffries?"

Jeffries was about to answer. But DeVille continued:

"Of course we are! We'd be delighted to accept. Two pints of *Old Hornblower*, if you please!"

"I thought you did an excellent job today. My defendant was guilty and the sentence was commensurate with his crimes, though I must confess it was something of an accident on my part!"

"Well, sometimes Providence plays its part," mused DeVille for a moment. And then he remembered where they were and called his protégé to the bar.

"Come on Jeffries, don't hang about lad, get the drinks in!"

In Coram's Fields

I knew very well the location DeVille was referring to. It was one of the regular haunts of my undergraduate days. Suffice to say Lamb's Conduit and its environs was on my beat. Yes, I knew Holborn and I knew the modern Babylonian ziggurat that was then, and I believe still is, a pile of flats and shops and hanging baskets.

This story begins with an arrest. A woman has stolen some meat from the local supermarket. Let's call her *Nancy*. There is an old boy who comes to the station to plead her case. He is perhaps her father but more likely her grand-father. We'll call him Tom, *Old Tom*. He explains that Nancy's husband has just got out of jail. She is at home with a couple of kids and has been doing the best for them whilst he's been inside. She's even managed to save a little money – enough to keep her old man (I'll call him Bill), in drink for a couple of weeks down at the 'Boar's Head'. Old Tom has come to trade. DeVille listens.

"Nancy needs to get away from him, permanently. She and the kids need somewhere safe to live!"

You have to remember that, in those day, there wasn't support generally available for battered wives and other victims of domestic violence, female or male. Nowadays we are more enlightened.

"I can tell you about a load of 50Ps. He's got thousands of forged coins stashed away in a lock-up".

"I tell you what," says DeVille, "I'll make some enquiries and see what I can do."

About half an hour later DeVille returns with some positive news.

"I've been talking to a bloke I know in Social Services. We can get her and the kids a place in North London."

"North London!", exclaimed Old Tom. But he realised beggars can't be choosers and Nancy needed to be away from the local area to be safe.

"Nancy never saw Bill after that – and never has, to the best of my knowledge. I used to keep in touch with Old Tom for a few years after, but I suppose he must have passed on," reflected DeVille.

But Bill saw me. He saw more of me than he ever wanted to. No amount of money, no number of 50P coins, could divert me from my path. We recovered over three-thousand forged coins – remember this was the 1970's, so it was no mean sum – and Bill went down for five years."

DeVille was in reflective mood and fell momentarily silent. He lit his customary small cigar and continued:

"Nowadays Nancy would never have been charged but in those days we followed a different procedure. Basically it was: *Touch-Arrest-Convict.* If you collared someone you had to arrest them, and if arrested then you had to make sure you had a very good chance of conviction. It was all written down in the old 12A[6], a huge bound tome with hand-written notes copper-plated by the duty Desk Sergeant. Today Nancy would have had recourse to a legitimate defence of extreme duress. On this occasion she was charged with theft, bailed, and summonsed to attend court some two to three weeks later. She received a fine and was given a supervision order for a first offence. And all because her husband was released from prison!"

Even though DeVille was able to help Nancy and bring Bill to book, it was clear that he still found the justice system's performance unsatisfactory, galling even. I think I agree.

---

[6] Also known as the 'Refused Charge Book'

A Tabloid Tale

It was the Sun what did it!

DeVille rang this morning. We had business to discuss and, inevitably, he had a story to tell. He was not sure if he had told me before but did I have a moment?

As I listened I realised I had heard this particular tale before but I could not recall the details. It was an exposition of observational curiosity and deductive brilliance. But I am not best placed to tell the story. Let me introduce you to another who was there at the time and learnt more than he had ever expected to learn on his first shift in a Q-Car. This was Detective Foster, now Chief Inspector Foster. He was DeVille's new apprentice that day.

As it happens, I am sitting waiting for Chief Inspector Foster to arrive. He is due in on a flight from New York, where he has been seconded with the NYPD Homicide Squad for the last couple of years. I am tucked into the window-corner of a country pub, overlooking the Thames not far from Oxford. Morse territory, you might say. We had arranged to meet so I could check some facts about the Q-Car case. At that time Foster was only recently appointed to C.I.D. He was straight out of college, or near enough. Having completed his obligatory stint in uniform he was, as expected, fast-tracked into the non-uniformed ranks. He had been assigned to shadow the detectives who were driving the station's single unmarked police vehicle that day. A spot of *out-&-about*, *see-what's-going-on*. A non-committal *stroll-on-wheels* in the local area. Foster was in the back of the car; seated in front were D.C. Saunders (driver) and D.S. DeVille (passenger). But here's Foster now – I'll let him continue:

'Yes. Thank you. Well it was my first full day with C.I.D. so I was a bit apprehensive, as you might expect, as well as very excited. As you say, I was detailed to shadow D.S. DeVille. I had been introduced the day before by our Desk Sergeant. DeVille welcomed me aboard and said:

"Just keep your eyes and ears open and you'll be fine! See you here tomorrow at 08:00 hours sharp."

I arrived at the station at least twenty minutes early the next day – more like half an hour, in fact. It felt strange to be in mufti. I hadn't known quite what to wear. I mean, my wardrobe wasn't very extensive. Should I take the Parker or maybe the duffle-coat? In the end I borrowed my flatmate's old RAF trench-coat. I needn't have worried as neither Saunders nor DeVille had pretensions as fashion icons. Saunders looked at me and said: *That'll do.* I considered that was approval enough, as much as I could expect, and we all went out into the yard together to collect the Q-Car. It would have been an old Wolseley back in the day, but that was at least twenty years before. This vehicle was a grey-coloured Austin Allegro. The car was inconspicuous enough; the three blokes crammed into it must have looked highly suspicious to even the most casual glance from a passing pedestrian.

"So what do you remember of that first day with C.I.D.?" I asked Foster, wanting him to go on. He paused a moment and I waited for him to continue in what had become a sort of mid-Atlantic accent.

"Well, I remember we got take-away coffees at the end of the High St. That's right, spilled most of mine on the back seat! Anyway, we had been driving around for about an hour or so when DeVille turned to Saunders and said:

"You see that blue saloon car by the hairdresser's shop? Let's just take a look, shall we?"

We drew up in front of the blue car – I think it might have been a Mercedes, I'm not sure. I got out of the car with DeVille and stood close behind him, listening intently and carefully observing everything that happened. *Eyes & Ears*, that's what he'd told me.

DeVille approached the driver seated behind the wheel and showed him his police badge. He asked if the car was his. It was. He asked if he might inspect the boot? No problem. We looked in the boot. Just a spare petrol can, empty, and a few loose cotton buds. I think I had been expecting to find a gangland corpse and felt a tad disappointed! DeVille closed the car boot. He looked in the back of the car, finding a *London A to Z* and a small spray-bottle of sealant, like that used for fixing drawings sketched in charcoal. No knives, no guns, no freshly minted bank notes. Nothing of interest at all, I thought.

"Right mate, you're nicked!" DeVille pronounced, "You don't have to say anything ..."

"Why are we arresting him?" I asked.

"Fraud," replied DeVille.

It was only later that I heard about DeVille's previous role as Police Liaison Officer with the Post Office Fraud Investigation Team (PrOFIT for short). It was what he had learnt while working with them that had triggered his radar, so to speak. He recognised some elements of a unique puzzle, one where he knew how all the pieces fitted together.

The owner of the car, with an almost empty boot and not much else, said nothing as we cuffed him and sat him down in the back of our Allegro. We drove back to the station to book him in for questioning.

Back at my desk I was reviewing the evidence. I could make very little of it. However, I did notice that the *A to Z* fell open at a particular page, seemingly well used. It had a few markings on it – red circles drawn in biro. I turned the next few pages and found similar markings. Perhaps they were indicating Off Licenses or Bookies? I suggested this to DeVille. He commended my observational skill and application. But he suggested I go for a walk and see if I could identify a couple of the places shown on the map. So I did. About an hour later I returned and went in search of DeVille. I found him in the staff canteen sipping at his coffee.

"Well?" he asked.

"I did what you said and they are all ..."

"Post Offices," interjected DeVille.

"Yes, how did you know?

"What, apart from my extensive knowledge of the local geography, you mean?" said DeVille.

"Oh I see."

"Well, to be fair, I had my suspicions. My geography isn't as good as that."

"What suspicions?"

"Well, do you remember our suspect was keen to bring his newspaper with him when we arrested him?"

"Yes, I remember. It was a tabloid, maybe the *Sun*?"

"Now when we arrived at the station he put it straight in the bin."

"Yes, I thought that was peculiar."

"And then D.C. Saunders called you back out to show you the return procedure for the Q-Car. Right?"

"Right."

"So let me tell you what happened next, what you *didn't* see."

DeVille proceeded to explain the devious means by which money may be illegally extracted from a Post Office Account.

Here is the list of ingredients you need, as related to me from memory by Foster:

1. Post Office Savings Book (preferably several);
2. Cotton Buds;
3. Fixer solution;
4. A John Bull printing set;
5. Map showing local Post Office branches;
6. A skill in forging signatures;
7 Nerve, lots of it.

The recipe itself reads something like this:

Redacted.[7]

Foster continued:

"DeVille had recognised some of the elements needed for this crime in the items found firstly in the car boot and secondly within the *A to Z*. However, it was when he asked to read the discarded newspaper that our suspect's pretence of innocent silence was finally revealed as nothing but pretence. As DeVille picked up the tabloid half a dozen Post Office Savings books fell out. He was not entirely surprised. He was though a little pleased with himself, as he readily admits.

He also told me that subsequently the Post Office Fraud Investigation Team discovered a sack-full of Savings books at the fraudster's home address. Apparently they had been looking for this character for the last eighteen months, but without success. Until now, that is. I don't know if they celebrated all night but, if they did, I'm sure DeVille would have been guest of honour!"

---

[7] Obviously the process is not given in detail so as not to provide a working guide for the would-be master fraudster. Thriller writers please take note when dealing with terrorist plots (Ed).

"Tell me," I asked, "how would you describe what, and how much, you learned from DeVille? Was he a strong influence on your professional development and on your career?"

"I'm glad you asked me that. The answer to both of those questions is: *Yes, most definitely*. There are two things I would say. Firstly he taught me the importance not only of careful observation but also of curiosity – the importance of looking for the links between observation, meaning and motive. A simple example is him asking me to follow up on the *A to Z* locations. You always need to ask: *What does this mean?* Secondly, and this is far less tangible, he taught me the virtue of honesty. When I started in the force there was still a level of corruption that had not yet been fully uncovered. His example and advice saved me from falling foul of that. I was young and inexperienced, innocent even. I could easily have fallen prey to the influence of less scrupulous senior officers' commands and demands. DeVille taught me the value of referring to my own moral compass by sharing his own."

I nodded in agreement, recognising this quality in DeVille from others I had spoken to.

I asked Foster if he knew what had happened when the case eventually came to court. He did not. Fortunately DeVille informed me some time later and I was able to fill in the details now for Foster's benefit. This is what I told him:

"DeVille told me that when the case finally came to court the accused did not attend. His Father had signed as surety for the accused and put up a £3000 bail. Now that the Bird had flown he erroneously assumed he could ask to be released from the surety and the bail fee. Much to his annoyance he found that, whilst he could be released from the surety, he was still liable for the bail, which he duly forfeited. The Bird? Flown where? Ireland. In the custody of the Guardia. On what charge? Defrauding the Irish Post Office."

"You couldn't make it up!" exclaimed Foster. And indeed you couldn't. The apogee of habitual offending, the exemplar *par excellence* of recidivism, as a learned Judge at the Old Bailey once said, as I recall, in a brief moment of clarity.

"But what I don't understand," I said, "is why DeVille stopped to inspect the blue saloon in the first place? Do *you* know why?"

Foster pondered for a moment, drawing pensively on his American cigarette:

"You know that's always puzzled me too. I did ask him and he did give me an answer – but I'm not sure I understand it."

"How do you mean?" I asked.

"When I pushed him on the point – why that particular blue saloon car, in that place, at that time, on that day, he just smiled and said:"

"Well now, that's between me and my God!"

I raised an eyebrow.

Foster raised his glass:

"I propose a toast," he declared:

To DeVille! May his long-suffering Confessor[8], if he has one, break his vows and explain to us the reason why!"

We clinked our glasses together, laughed loudly, and drank up.

"Time Gentlemen please," called the landlord.

---

[8] I mentioned to Foster that I have an outstanding query with Father Columba.

Given A Chance

DeVille seemed to embrace a fairly pragmatic philosophy, one designed to get results in the short term but with the potential for benefits in the longer term also. He would typically give people a chance to help themselves. That is not to say he was susceptible to bribes. Absolutely not. When asked how much to '*make it go away*' (whatever misdemeanor it might be) he would estimate: "Oh about £70,000 pounds, I'd say! Or you could just pay the fine – for not having a valid M.O.T. certificate it's about £25, if I remember correctly." The following examples illustrate his philosophy in practice:

The Theobald Family:

Policemen need their informers. Sometimes these informers are inspired not so much by money as by brotherly love. Or, in this instance, and to be more accurate, by sisterly love. A sister snitches on her brother and her brother gives up his two mates. Yes, together they did the burglary at *The Larches*; yes, they took the jewellery and various other items. What had they done with the loot? They'd passed it on already. Where to? An address on the edge of the common.

DeVille spoke to his colleague Saunders. They would pay a visit. The main objective was to retrieve the uninsured jewellery on behalf of the elderly couple at *The Larches*.

By the time they were ready to proceed it was late Saturday morning. As they approached along the high lane the first thing DeVille noticed was something curious in the front garden. Gradually he made out lots of flowers displayed on the lawn in a round. Slowly it dawned on him that these were actually wreaths. Duly noted.

DeVille knocks on the door. A man dressed in a black suit and tie opens it.

"Can we speak to Mr Timothy Theobald?"

"Yes, that's me. What do you want? I'm burying my Dad in an hour's time!

"I'll come straight to the point, Sir. I understand you bought some jewellery recently – I'm afraid it was stolen. I realise you wouldn't have known that but we need you to give it back. I need it returned to the Police Station by half past three this afternoon, no questions asked."

"Yes, fine, three-thirty, I understand."

DeVille could see the parlour was already full of people, attending the wake, some twenty or thirty rough looking 'ne'er-do-wells', you might say. In the circumstances he thought it best to retire gracefully – he was familiar with the saying concerning discretion and valour.

"Cor, you let him off lightly!" said Saunders.

"Yes, I know but the coffin was in the parlour. There's a time and a place – and that was neither", replied DeVille.

Come half-past three – nothing. DeVille waits. At four o'clock he calls Theobald.

"Mr Theobald, you haven't delivered the jewellery as agreed? I thought we had an agreement?

"Who the hell are you!"

"Mr Theobald, please don't mess me about … He's hung up!"

Young Billy, keen as mustard to impress in his first days on probation with CID, says to DeVille: "Let's get a riot team and all of Melsham Police Station down there – we can sort them out!"

Back to the common. Timothy Theobald answers the door once again. There is no-one in the parlour. Old Mr Theobald is underground and his family, friends, and any other acquaintances, have now departed (though perhaps not so finally).

"What agreement? We didn't agree nuffin'. Get lost!"

A size twelve brogue wedges the door as Theobald tries to slam it shut (Saunders is abusing his finely polished leather shoes but it is all in a good cause).

"Right, you're nicked!" exclaims DeVille.

Then his younger brother appears.

"I advise you to step back," says DeVille, but he didn't.

And then there were two nicked.

Timothy's wife appears, hollering and screaming and shouting abuse.

That's three nicked!

DeVille would not be going to the theatre with his wife that evening after all. He'd have to make it up to her another time.

"It was clear that the jewellery was no longer in the house or thereabouts any more. Our objective was still to get the jewellery back," DeVille explained.

That afternoon the Station Desk Sergeant finds himself somewhat busier than usual. Timothy Theobald's cousin is making too much noise. The Desk Sergeant nicks him.

And that makes four nicked on the day of the funeral. All four banged up courtesy of Her Majesty's Government. Only Mr Theobald Senior keeps his silence.

On the Sunday, around about mid-day, DeVille gets a call from the Duty Sergeant.

"That lot we've got locked up in the cells – someone's delivered a box of jewellery. Said you'd understand. Can you drop by and sort this out?"

It transpired that all the missing jewellery was in that box, plus a load of other stuff from other burglaries! Timothy Theobald was charged with handling stolen property. He spent two years in Wandsworth prison at Her Majesty's pleasure.

"What about the deal we had?" cried Theobald.

"Look, you ruined my evening at the theatre – and your own father's funeral – no deal mate!"

"I would have held my side of the bargain" said DeVille, "but he blew his chance".

The Plumber:

"It was in the Regent St. area. All round there was designed by Thomas Nash. His patron was the Prince Regent, later King George III. Nash's architecture rivals even that of Hawksmoor and Wren, you know". I had noticed before that DeVille seemed to have a genuine interest in the buildings and history of London. He wore his knowledge lightly but liked to share it when it might be appreciated.

"Her father was in oil. An Oil Magnate. His daughter was in her mid-twenties, I'd say. Nice girl, very polite – offered us cups of tea. Anyway, she'd called a plumber to fix a leaking toilet. The plumber duly arrives and fixes it in about five minutes – no more than ten – and charges an extortionate fee. Nothing unusual in that, you might say. And you'd be right. Of course it's different nowadays when we've got loads of Polish plumbers. Do a good job too and nowhere near so expensive."

"So why are you telling us about this plumber. What happened that made you remember him?" I asked.

"Ah yes, the plumber. Shortly after he finishes the job and leaves, she discovers that her watch is missing. Yes it was valuable – diamond encrusted etc. – but more than that it was a twenty-first birthday present from father.

I decided we'd call the same firm and get the same plumber. I thought we might just pull his ball-cock, so to speak! As it happened that wasn't necessary. He squealed like a pig in pepper.

'I think you've flushed your last toilet, matey!' I said.

'This watch you nicked is worth a lot of money. If we charge you you'll go to prison – it's twenty-five grand's worth!

If we get it back we might be able to do a deal, but you will still be charged. We can put in a good word for you with the Magistrate – co-operative and all that – but it will have to go "up the road" – and probably as far as Inverness![9]

'So who've you sold it to then?'

'He'll kill me if I tell you!'

'What makes you think *I* won't?' said DeVille slowly and deliberately, smiling sideways at young Billy.

'I sold it to that bloke who runs the Café down on Mortimer Street!'

He'd sold it for fifty quid. I paid a visit to the Café down on Mortimer Street. I spoke to the owner and explained that – he wouldn't have known it – but the watch he bought was stolen. Obviously he was told it came from the seller's Grandmother. Unfortunately that wasn't true. All the guy needed to say was: "Yeah, that's right." But he said nothing. I tried a different tack:

'Okay. How long have you had this Café? How much longer do you *want* to have it? If you're convicted ...'

We all laughed. DeVille paused to savour the moment.

"Needless to say we got the watch back and he carried on producing his famous sausage & black pudding sandwiches!

The plumber? He got six months."

---

[9] The meaning of this expression remains unclear but is authentic (Ed.)

Operation Seaside

I have received a scrap, a fragment, of information from DeVille in a *txt msg*. It mentions the suspects are builders from Worthing and Littlehampton. It mentions prostitutes and murder. I am eager to know more.

DeVille talks of the murder of a dominatrix somewhere in West London. His witness is a fellow practitioner of the art. I am eager to know more about the case. Should I give him a ring and ask him to add some flesh to the bare bones? Isn't that just asking for trouble? Yes, it is. I call him:

"*Pronto!*"

DeVille is in an Italian mood.

"*Com es tai?*" I counter promptly.

"*Si, si, va bene?*"

I revert to the vernacular.

"I got your text. Are you busy now?"

"No, that's fine. You want to know the details, I presume?"

"Yes please", I answered.

"Well, it was like this. Recently I spoke to an ex-colleague. I happened to mention the story of the two builders who killed a prostitute. He thought it was worth writing up. Let me tell you what I told him:

A prostitute was murdered in a flat one weekend – probably on the Sunday. The Police were called about midnight. She was found tied up in the bath. The P.M. confirmed drowning."

"The P.M.?" I asked.

Yes, the *post mortem*. We got the team together. There was myself and Cliff, both plainclothes, and young Ronnie, an East End boy who fancied himself as a bit of a wonder-kid in the world of detection. He was doing his probation. We were led by Detective Inspector Paddy Mulvaney. The D.I. was what you might call a character, a bit eccentric even – he used to come to work on a push-bike, complete with cycle clips and a pair of rabbit-skin gauntlets. Mind you, nobody ever mentioned it. He was an excellent copper: he was fair, he was thorough, and he got results – taught me a lot.

So the team make a start: we ID the victim, make a list of known associates, note the deceased's profession and do an 'ANACAPA' – i.e. link up all the different people, places, times, sightings, etc. in a graphic network, drawn up on a board, as it was in those days. Of course it'd all be computerised nowadays."

"Yes, I've seen the sort of thing used by Customs and Excise when tracking smugglers and traffickers. I think they do the same to monitor potential terrorists as well?"

"Yes, that's right. So you know what I mean then. Anyway, we pay a visit to a potential witness. This was about three weeks after the murder. Another working girl – not so much a Lady of the Night as a Lady of the Day, working from home in a purpose-built room – well more like a dungeon really."

"I get the picture," I said. "Go on."

"Well, we've confirmed that certain items are missing from the flat: there's no jewellery, no cash, no music station or TV. Clearly she's been robbed as well as killed. Anyway, we identified a friend of the deceased, someone in a similar line of business, you might say. She worked from home and had a maid to keep the place clean and tidy. We ring the doorbell and the maid answers, leading us into the front parlour."

"Please sit down. Miss Zaria will be through in a moment."

"After a few moments Miss Zaria enters in a wasp basque, wearing high-heels with fish-net stockings, carrying a riding crop, and sporting a rather revealing top-piece with peek-a-boo bra cups. Neither Paddy nor I bat an eyelid. Young Ronnie, however, is completely agog! Then the phone rings. Miss Zaria is expecting another client very soon. We've got five minutes.

'You must be here about Sindy?'

'That's right,' says Paddy.

Most people in her line of work are not usually very forthcoming but Paddy was well known and well respected in these parts. He had credibility. A couple of years back he had put away a pimp, a nasty piece of work, who had been beating up some of the local girls. But that's another story and probably best told by Paddy himself.

Then we hear the client arrive and it looks like our five minutes are up. We hear the maid usher him into the other room.

Miss Zaria says: 'I'll be back in just a mo' dears.' The next thing is we hear whacking and screaming from next door! Ronnie's face is an absolute picture – like a portrait by Picasso."

Miss Zaria returns to the parlour where we are sitting.

'He'll be ok for a little while,' she said.

I was certain I saw Miss Zaria wink at Paddy. They were up to something. At that point she turns to Ronnie, who is still catching flies with his mouth wide open, and points at his feet with her riding crop:

'Detective, your shoes aren't very clean – take them off and we'll have them spick and span in no time,' she smiled persuasively.

Ronnie does as he's told. She goes next door, carrying the shoes in one hand and her riding crop in the other. The next we hear is:

'Whack! Look at these shoes! Lick them clean! I want them spotless!'

After that Ronnie never came into work without his shoes spotlessly clean and polished to the very highest standard. He even surpassed Saunders who, as you know, was ex-military and the epitome of perfection in the gentlemen's footwear department!

Anyway, from our little *tete a tete* with Miss Zaria we manage to ID two suspects: Bertie & Bob, two itinerant builders. It just so happened that the victim had recently had a special room built, a sort of chamber for entertaining guests. Bertie and Bob had been hired for the job. They were specialists in this sort of work – cash in hand, no questions asked."

I was about to ask DeVille what he thought their motive might be but he continued:

"Incidentally, most of these women were not sex workers, as such. They traded in S&M and catering for fetishes of one sort or another – they were mostly lesbians."

I had heard DeVille express this view before and was not surprised to hear him repeat it. Whether it were true, or not, I had no way of knowing but I did know that this was not a view that could be readily expressed in today's more enlightened climate. However, there are some well documented facts that have come to the attention of the authorities. For example, today the capital is flooded with prostitutes from the old Eastern Bloc countries, especially Romania. How many of these girls are trafficked it is impossible to say. A Parliamentary Committee is currently investigating this. However, I suspect the position of Dominatrix remains very much a British vocation. DeVille continued:

"So now we had identified two likely lads. They already had form. One had been charged with gross indecency and both had convictions for burglary. But there was no history of violence. If we could trace the stolen property we might get somewhere. Unfortunately we only knew it was missing by its absence and had no specific description of it. How should we play it, given the circumstances? Chief Inspector Bailey, who had assumed overall control of *Operation Seaside*, decided we should go and pick 'em up and see what we could sweat out of 'em.

We set up two operational teams. One would go to Littlehampton and the other would go to Worthing. I was sent to Worthing with Cliff, another detective sergeant who I'd worked with successfully before. Good bloke. Very funny. Only not so good at covering your back because he always liked to be in front. Paddy meanwhile took Littlehampton.

We located and nicked the two suspects, no problem, and bagged some shoes and clothing. Then we accompanied them back to London for further questioning. In those days we were able to detain suspects longer than twenty-four hours. That was before the *Police and Criminal Evidence Act*, or 'PLAICE' as it was known *unoffishally*. Nowadays, with the advent of the Crown Prosecution Service (CPS)[10] and its focus on the *statistics of success*, the Police have to have assembled far more evidence before making an arrest. In some cases this is unrealistic, especially when time is of the essence, and doesn't always help with a successful prosecution," DeVille commented.

I could see what he was driving at but I wasn't sure whether it was a justifiable criticism or merely a typical response to change – perhaps it was a bit of both. If you've been in the same line of business, or the same organisation, for some time you start to see that things go round in circles – this is called, variously: progress,

---

[10] a.k.a. Criminal Protection Society

improvement, transformation, or a bloody nuisance! One day the old way of doing things comes right back into fashion, though it is bound to be given a new name when it does! DeVille nodded in agreement.

But let's get back to the story, DeVille's expanded and ever expanding account of the Worthing operation, including the arrest and questioning of some key witnesses:

"As a result of our questioning we established that an alibi needed checking. Also we needed more background on the two suspects. To do this we had to go back down to the coast.

We arrived at our modest hotel. It had the necessary Telex machine for communications with H.Q – remember, this was in the days before computers, mobile phones, or even fax machines. It was in a side street close to, but not on, the seafront. The receptionist asked me

"Do you want (a) paper?"

"I was rather hoping for sheets and a blanket," I replied.

"Sorry, I mean a newspaper."

Cliff groaned at my attempt at spontaneous humour. He said he hoped I would keep my comical efforts to a minimum during our stay – probably best leave the jokes to him, in fact. Cliff was recognised by Scotland Yard for his Tommy Cooper impersonations. In fact he could have been his twin. At one Office Christmas Party we provided him with a fez to complete the picture. I once asked him how he managed to do such a fantastic impression. *"Just like that!"* he said – I should have seen that one coming.

Anyway, the following morning we met up with the local CID. We went to a flat to interview the potential witnesses, two couples. However, they were all a bit worse for wear – the evidence of the previous night's party still clear for anyone to see. We suggested they sober up, freshen up, and come and see us at the Station later that afternoon. We wanted to talk to them about a murder that had taken place a few weeks previously up in the Smoke[11]. Of course we knew that by then they would have agreed on what they were going to say.

At three p.m. the two couples arrive at the Station. The bloke

---

[11] i.e. London (Ed.)

who owned the flat was a bit 'gobby', you might say, and obviously not a fan of us coppers. After a little while he finally said to Cliff:

'We don't know nuffink about nuffink, so we're going!'

'You know we've came from a long way to see you?'

'Yeah, so what?'

All of a sudden Cliff has got hold of his shirt and jacket and has hauled him over the desk.

'Right, you're nicked for wasting police time, obstruction and attempting to pervert the course of justice![12]'

This little episode had the desired effect. All three of his friends had seen what had just happened. Cliff knew exactly what he was doing and so it would prove when it came to the individual interviews."

DeVille split them up – each being interviewed separately – and proceeded to question one of the women in an adjacent room. I watch, like a fly on the wall, as he employs the *You know that I know that you know …* method (one taught him by D.I. Mulvaney)

"I could see from her demeanour she knew more about what we were talking about than she was letting on," he explained. Eventually she said that her friend told her Bertie had boasted about killing someone, though she didn't know who and he was always boasting so they never took him seriously. DeVille took note. This was a breakthrough at last. He needed to corroborate this new information. DeVille continues:

"I moved on to the next witness, the other girl on the group. She confirmed what her friend had said. Or rather she said her friend had told her about the boast. This was good enough. I knew then we had them."

But DeVille still needed to crack the suspects' alibi. Their version of the timeline of events had them visiting the flat in Worthing mid-afternoon on the Sunday. This would have meant that they could not have committed the murder in London that same afternoon. He manoeuvred around the subject, until he came to the matter of what was on television that afternoon, about teatime. It was Attenborough's *Blue Planet*. Now the witness was absolutely adamant that he never missed an episode of this programme and his friends, Bertie and Bob, had not been

---

[12] Known as an "over the counter" arrest.

with him at this time. They were there in the evening but they must have arrived later and not before about seven o'clock. This was the second key piece of evidence.

"So what was the third key piece of evidence?" I asked, knowing that things always come in threes.

"Funny you should ask that. It was a false trail that the culprits had laid later that afternoon. They had been in a Video Rental shop and deliberately knocked over a stand. They had made sure the store manager noticed and even helped pick up the cassette cases from the floor. They said they had to get back to watch a programme on television – *Blue Planet*. When interviewed the store manager remembered this but not the time of the incident. He assumed it was later in the afternoon than it actually was. And that was the third key piece of evidence."

By this time we've been talking on the phone for about thirty to forty minutes and I still don't know the motive for the murder – DeVille interrupts himself to ask:

"Am I taking too long?"

I reassure him that he isn't, though this may not be the truth, the whole truth, and nothing but the truth.

"There's just one more thing I must tell you about," said DeVille.

"Go on," I said, realising we were on a roll here.

"The local liaison officers had been very helpful to us and our Guv says take 'em out for a meal and he'll sort out the expenses. So we do. We asked for a recommendation – somewhere good to eat, and drink.

'What do you want to eat? Do you like Middle Eastern food?" We've got a very nice little Armenian Restaurant in town. It's only about five minutes walk.'

So off we go. There are about six of us altogether.

As we enter I am surprised to be addressed in person by a familiar voice."

'Welcome Mr Deevil, Sir! So good to see you again. Your usual table with the all-round view?'

Faisal! How are you?"

They shake hands, each gripping strongly and neither letting go for a while.

'This is my cousin's restaurant – him I'm helping out – we can say assisting?' explains Faisal.

Faisal was a small West End restaurant owner and Scotland Yard had used his premises as a de-brief venue on the [XXX] enquiry and several other less well-known cases. Faisal was a great collector of all idioms of the English vernacular and was proud to practice them whenever he could – sometimes with curious results ...

'Still drinking the French wine Mr Deevil Sir? So good, so good. Drinks are on top of the house! We hope to see you under the table, this best table, in the later evening!'

DeVille acknowledged Faisal's greeting and accepted the table he guided them to, set back from the window but with a good view of all exits and entrances. DeVille was worried that the local team might be a bit put out.

'So you know Faisal?' they asked. 'What exactly are the odds on that?'

"Pretty long odds, I should think! But of course we are from Scotland Yard you know," said DeVille, in a what he hoped was a sufficiently self-deprecating tone.

[the following section has been redacted as it refers to the XXX enquiry (see above) which is subject to Scotland Yard's Fifty Year Rule[13]]

Finally I brought DeVille back to the question of motive. Why had these bungling builders committed the murder in the first place?

He told me that they had been involved in doing similar work for several customers, including the victim's lover, Eliza Enriques. She made a comment at some point. Something to the effect: 'I wish someone would just let her have it!'

Eliza Enriques was acquitted but the builders each got twenty-five years and won't be out again till they're near retirement age. Was she using them? Definitely. Did she get off scot free? Yes, she did. She was practised in the arts of persuasion, manipulation and domination. She had them under her heel. They didn't stand a chance."

---

[13] I can find no reference to this specifically but there is a U.K. Government Thirty Year Rule. In addition certain matters are prevented from disclosure under the Official Secrets Act (Ed.)

DeVille finished his story at last. Then he revealed something of himself that seemed rather interesting. He said:

"You know, when I was telling that story I felt I was actually sitting in that room, with Ronnie to the left, and Paddy opposite, and the maid comes in with the bottle of *Courvoisier* and some large brandy glasses ..."

On Interviewing Considered as One of the Fine Arts

Coincidence occurs occasionally, but it is the exception rather than the rule. DeVille's assumption is that it is only coincidence if it cannot be proven otherwise. In other words his temperament is sceptical, though not cynical. DeVille believes in a balance of probabilities and, more often than not, that balance falls in favour of connection rather than coincidence. This particular case was no exception. The deaths of two elderly neighbours within the space of just under six months was certainly suspicious. Further investigation confirmed due cause for suspicion.

The first incident concerned the stabbing of an elderly lady who lived on her own. Although there were no obvious signs of anything having been stolen, it was known that she had been keeping the Christmas Kitty for the local Pensioners Club, of which no sign was found. In fact no cash was found in the flat at all, save for a few coppers in her purse. Clearly this was a case of murder. Someone had wielded the knife, though the weapon itself had not been found.

The second incident concerned an elderly gentleman. He lived in the same block of flats; he was found dead at the bottom of the stairs. Perhaps he had fallen? However, his son was not convinced. His view was supported by the fact that the front door to his flat was not locked. His Father never left his flat without locking the door behind him, not even if he were just putting out the rubbish. But that was not all. In his pocket was a receipt for a betting slip. Enquiries at the local Bookie's revealed significant winnings – more than one hundred pounds. However, there was no sign of the cash in the flat.

DeVille began:

"It is a well-known fact, supported by a wealth of statistical evidence, that the majority of murderers are known to their victims. Killings at random, by total strangers, are very rare.

Where they do occur they often come about as a result of a botched burglary, or the like. In both of these particular cases theft was suspected. If so then how had the thief (or thieves) gained access to the properties? Was there a common *modus operandi* that might indicate a single culprit?"

DeVille pondered these matters.

"Further enquiries led to a suspect fitting the frame. He lived in the same block of flats. He had a habit to feed. The evidence was circumstantial – there was no DNA found and there were no finger-prints found – but I decided to bring him in for questioning anyway. Perhaps applying a bit of pressure would produce results."

At this point, DeVille tells us, we need to be made aware of the *un*official practices associated with interviewing suspects, in addition to the better known official procedures. As well as formal recordings, with timings and stating who is present at interview, other detectives may observe. Such observation may be from behind a two-way mirror or, if that is beyond the building's equipment budget, then over an internal audio system. This itself is nothing unusual.

"However, a little spice can always be added to the occasion by way of a small bet – nothing too extravagant, you understand. In this case some bottles of finest Scottish malt whisky. This is how it works:

The interviewer is given six random words that he must introduce into his questioning in the most natural and appropriate manner. For every word that he includes, and repeats at least three times, he wins a bottle of the finest Scottish malt whisky. There are six bottles in all that may be won. Failure to succeed in repetition of at least one word-triplicate means the tables are turned and the interviewer has to pay for an evening of drinks at the bar. Simple as that. Of course the words have to be relevant to the specific line of enquiry so you need to do your homework on the suspect first. I mean you had to know something about his background as well as the details of the case you were investigating. In this particular case the perpetrator would have been covered in blood, for example. The pathologist also told us that the knife wounds were few and precise."

Here is a transcript[14] of the interview conducted by DeVille on this occasion:

Time 14:45
Date xxxxxxxxxxxxxxx
Present XXXXXXXXXX XXXXXX XXXXXXXX

Ref: 0642 MT/07

D. So tell me, Mr Jarrod, where do you keep your clothes-pegs?
J. Clothes-pegs? I don't have any.

D. I see. So how do you dry your socks then?
J. My socks? I put them on the radiator.

D. Do you have central-heating?
J. Yes. All the flats do. There's a service boiler in the basement.

D. Right. And where's your local launderette?
J. I don't know. I don't use one.

D. So what about a washing-machine? Have you got a washing machine?
J. No. I wash my clothes by hand.

D. So when is washing day then?
J. Whenever I need to do some washing. No special day.

D. You were in the Army weren't you?
J. Err yes. I was.

D. Did you ever train to use a parachute?
J. No, I didn't.

D. But you were in the commandos, weren't you?
J. Well yes, but ...

---

[14] Parts of the transcript have been redacted as required under GDPR (Ed.)

D. So you were trained how to use a knife, I presume, I mean a commando knife?
J. Well yes, but we also used standard bayonets. I mean, I didn't get into the commandos in the end

D. Was that because you didn't complete the parachute training?
J. If you like.

D. Did you learn how to pack a parachute?
J. Well yes, but I never actually used one. I never did a jump.

D. And did you learn how to use your commando knife to cut yourself from a parachute if you landed in a tree?
J. I was able to do lots of things. I used it to open ration tins sometimes.
D. So would you say you were pretty handy with a knife then?

VVV......WW......... XXVVV
VVVX......WXW......... XXVVV

Unfortunately, as you can see from the torn sheet above, we do not have the entire record of the interview. The final pages of the transcript are missing from the file. Suffice to say that other random words known to have been included in the session, according to DeVille, were: *Cart-wheel, Parachute, Hamster,* and *Commando Knife–* wait a minute, that's only another four. So what was the fifth one? Ah yes, it's there in the transcript – I see it now – *Washing-machine.*

It will come as a surprise to no-one, I am sure, to learn that on completion of the interview DeVille had acquired all six bottles for his drinks cabinet-*cum*-cellar. Unlike fine wines, however, which are often laid down for posterity in order to acquire a unique patina and a more refined flavour, no dust was ever allowed to settle on these particular bottles, examples of the finest Scottish malt whisky!

Pandora's Box

We are in a railway town. There are former workers' cottages surrounding the main-lines and sidings and, surrounding them, vast post-war housing estates of multi-levelled red-brick blocks, like the impossibly piled-high passenger cabins of an ocean liner. We are docked in a siding not far from the centre of town. Here there are the ubiquitous fast-food outlets and charity shops, the scratch Estate Agents offices and the unashamed pawnbrokers shops, which stand alongside the ever-popular bargain pound shops.

I seek out the Chemist's in search of aspirin; the bright sunshine is penetrating the defence of my reactive glasses as the story bangs persistently at the windows of my will to write. I must write. I must complete the commission that has not been commissioned, the task that has not been allocated, the narrative that has not been captured. Here, in another otherwise disregarded but once important railway town, I must begin to assemble the pieces, apportion the elements, construct the boiler plate and pistons of another narrative that is not my own. Let us begin:

There is a murder. It is witnessed. Some witnesses report seeing a stabbing. As it happens the victim was not stabbed though he was murdered. The incident was reported – the killing of the man. As it happened he was shot but that was not clear until later, much later. The body disappeared, together with the drugs he had been casually distributing. Later the body was found – or more precisely parts of it were found. The first part was the (headless) torso (legless). The suspect was a member of the gypsy fraternity, as it happened. The motive for murder was unclear; it may simply have been a disagreement about some trivial matter; it may have been about supplying drugs – perhaps the *perp*[15] had a sister who had died of an overdose? Whatever the

---

[15] Perpetrator (Ed.)

motive, the dealer was dead and so far only his torso had been found.

DeVille was assigned to the task and immediately realised there were pieces to this unique puzzle that were missing: e.g. head, arms, legs etc. He started to make enquiries. He was diligent, he was persistent, he was lucky no doubt. The identity of the suspect was quickly revealed. He had gone into hiding and then he had been arrested and put into gaol. He was due to appear before the local Magistrates. As this was an indictable offence they would of course refer the case to the criminal court. Their own remit was more circumscribed and parochial but they served the Law nonetheless. The suspect was held in cells over the weekend – a Bank Holiday weekend, as it happened. But he did not remain there for the duration. Sometime on the Friday evening he walked out unchallenged and went to visit a friend. This was not a good move as his circle of friends was well known and, very soon, DeVille was knocking on the door of a small cottage on the western edge of Melsham Common.

Before I continue I must say something more about the Box. I think mentioned it earlier and, after all, it is the title of this piece. It is fundamental to DeVille's stories and to his recounting them. Usually it is kept closed. This is probably for reasons of safety. If he does not need to open the Box then DeVille prefers not to do so. Or so he says. Whilst he is able to maintain his comic flight in relating tales of his professional experience, he does so. But occasionally, very occasionally, the Box is opened – albeit briefly – and another reality escapes before some temporary semblance of order is restored and chaos returns to its cage. Of course *humour* is the key, the key to maintaining a semblance of sanity. For the while the Box remains firmly closed; it is locked and sealed; it is unopened. We shall return later, when DeVille isn't looking, when he is lulled into that false sense of security which deceives us all at some time or another.

The court – it is a Magistrates Court – is quite embarrassed. It has lost its composure, most likely, and it has lost its remanded prisoner most certainly. What must it do? It must find him immediately and return him to custody. Then it must review the slackness of its own holding procedures on Bank Holiday weekends. There will be someone's guts going for garters!

So, we are on the western edge of Melsham Common. There is

a small cottage, approached by a half-made driveway of cinder and brick. An approximate avenue of beech and box hedge lines the approach. The cottage stands on its own near a small lake. It was once, perhaps, a woodsman's cottage or a gamekeeper's house. Now it is in need of repair and black smoke oozes intermittently from an oddly angled chimney stack. We knock firmly on the door and, before it creeps open even an inch, we smash it down with a two-person, double-handled, battering-ram, leaving a trail of painted shards and wooden splinters. DeVille leads:

"Don't mind if we come in now, do we?"

"What the ..."

"No? Very sensible."

DeVille marches comfortably through the hallway and into the living-room; his eyes skirt around the edges of the room, scanning for exits and entrances, for tell tale signs of mugs, smouldering cigarette ends, and the like. He notices the meter, but we'll come back to that in a moment. There is no sign of our wanted man. No, he hasn't seen him lately. No, he hasn't been in touch. And yes, if he does get in touch, he'll call us straightaway.

"And you will tell us if you're planning anymore Cocktail Parties, I presume?"

"Sorry, what? Cocktail Parties?"

"Yes, that's right, Cocktail Parties."

DeVille directs his gaze at the electricity meter in the hallway, located just above the front door. I follow his gaze and peer at the black bakelite casing and the wheels within that turn almost imperceptibly. Now I see there is a reason that its spinning is almost halted and undetectable to the human eye. But the acute vision of DeVille has spotted something. In the side of the casing is a small hole; in the small hole is wedged a small stick; and the small stick retards the motion of the wheel. Minutes, hours and days tick by but the meter hardly moves; its lower numbers tumble only very occasionally, the larger ones not at all.

And the small matter of the shattered front-door? DeVille strikes a bargain. He is fair even when scrupulous. He is of the Law – neither above nor below it. He knows the Law and he uses the Law to meet its purpose. On this occasion he agrees to turn a blind eye to the electrical misdemeanour but only on one condition: that he is informed immediately of the escapee's whereabouts, should it become known. This is readily agreed to. Without question. Absolutely. No problem.

We leave. The search continues. Then, on the Monday evening, our itinerant fugitive returns to court. He has been missing the comforts of his cell and is in need of a good night's rest; alternatively, he is seeking sanctuary from a number of irate fellows who are in hot pursuit for some double-dealing he has arranged or some dubious tip he has given. No-one is more surprised, on the Tuesday morning, to see our man in court once more, hair-combed and freshly shaven, than the three Magistrates. Let us call our magistrates Shadrach, Meshach and Abednego. Meshach is the most senior among them and sits in the middle; Shadrach is older and slightly deaf in his right ear – he sits to the left of Meshach; Abednego is keen and eager and only recently qualified – a relative youngster at only forty-five. For a moment Magistrate Meshach thinks perhaps it was all just a bad dream, brought on by too much port at the Annual Golf Club Dinner on Friday night. There had been *no* escape. They had *not* lost their prisoner. It was just a trick sprung from his over-wrought brain. He turned to his fellow wise-persons. They also were surprised but confirmed that they also had been given to understand that the whereabouts of the person stood before them now was unknown. But explanations –if that's what they were – would have to wait till later. Together they had entered the furnace of judgement and despite uncertainty, and bolstered only by their faith in the Law, together they had survived. And now to work. Due consideration must be given, decisions arrived at, and (occasionally) arguments listened to. This fellow is destined for a higher court. Quite possibly the Old Bailey itself.

But there is a puzzle, even if we do not have all the pieces yet. So far we have only a torso. It is found floating in a lake in Surrey just south of the M25. It is wrapped in a black bin-liner. It has floated to the surface where an early morning dog-walker, or idly curious fisherman, has come upon it, quite by accident, at the water's edge.

At this point we can imagine how it is almost certainly best to keep images of swollen and rotting body parts firmly locked away in a box. There they may be retrieved and inspected by coroners and medical students alike, but where we may be spared the sight and the smell. DeVille also keeps them in the Box but when, as now, they must surface and retrace their steps, he makes light of things, as if mere trivia in a tale of much darkness.

Deville receives a note. The note says that Head Office have received a complaint. A bill has been submitted for the repair of a front door. One that was needlessly smashed by some over-zealous policemen knocking on the door with undue force.

I watch now as DeVille makes a call. It is to the General Electricity Board. Is someone available to carry out an inspection? Yes, a domestic property. Suspected abstraction of electricity. They meet outside the pub on the green. The King's Oak. Each introduces himself. DeVille leads the way, followed by the General Electricity Board and two uniformed officers. DeVille knocks. Forcefully. The newly repaired door gives way once more to his gentle persuasion and springs from its hinges like a carapace cracking off a turtle's back. Sure enough this cottage has been hosting more cocktail parties since our last visit. The wheel of the meter in the black bakelite casing is still, unmoving, arrested by a small stick stuck into a small hole in the side of the casing. Action is taken. An arrest is made. General Electricity Board, alone permitted to interfere with the Utility, either for the sake of safety or in the service of the Law, turns off the power supply to the property and makes safe. He writes a note in his official work book to call the National Gas Board. There might be need of a further inspection.

Meanwhile recovery of the several missing parts to this curious case is progressing apace. Legs have been located, or rather the location of the legs has been specified. A team of specialists is quickly assembled and, in a field no more than a mile from the old Dorking bypass, they set to work. It is about three months since the victim disappeared[16].

The field is down a rough and rutted track, strewn with flints. At the end of the track, at the near edge of the field, is an open shed or shelter of some kind. Hiding from the heat of the day are two ponies, a roan and a grey, both geldings. In the far bottom corner of the field are two more ponies, fidgeting and flicking at persistent flies.

---

[16] DeVille is at this time reprimanded by D.I. Kirkwall as he is at present on "light duties" because of a recent health alert (Ed.)

DeVille watches as the SOCO specialists[17] lead the ponies from the shelter and rig an electric fence around it, establishing a working area of about five or six metres in diameter. Seated in the police transport vehicle, outside of the circle, is an accomplice to our murderer and he is adamant that this is where he got rid of the legs. Buried them just a couple of feet below the surface. A couple of feet at most, no more.

The ground appears undisturbed. It is unlikely that anything is buried here. After more than an hour's careful attention to the stable floor, the SOCOs are certain there's nothing there. But DeVille persists. He has a hunch. And it is only a hunch. He persists, persuading them to return to the dig again and again.

"Can you give it just another ten minutes, lads?"

They continue: once, twice, three times and more, and finally, at an unexpected depth of precisely sixty-eight and a half inches (*however many centimetres that is*) they come across the first signs: a scrap of denim, then a blackened big-toe poking out from a red woollen sock. Carefully they remove the soil to discover a complete pair of legs. The pieces are starting to come together.

"So how come the scene seemed so unpromising and the legs were found at the depth almost six feet?" I asked.

"The ponies. They sleep standing up. They casually stomp the ground. Occasionally they may rest just one leg but they eventually trample the ground so much that it becomes like concrete in dry weather," DeVille replied.

"About six months later I was investigating another case. Armed robbery it was. It was a bad job. Some young lad in the wrong place at the wrong time. Got it straight in the belly. Bled out. Horrible way to go," DeVille continued.

Then he halted for a moment, as if re-encountering some aspect of the past he did not share directly, but uttered somehow as if to himself alone. I glimpsed the lid of the Box slightly ajar, something had slipped out from it and crept surreptitiously into the present.

"Anyway, we[18] were visiting the Morgue over at Deptford. Accompanying a grieving relative. Necessary identification procedure. You know the sort of thing."

---

[17] Scene of Crime Officers (SOCO)
[18] The body was in fact recognised by D.I. Kirkwall. (DeVille)

I didn't but could imagine. I mean, I could imagine the procedure, its formal necessity, but I could not imagine having to identify someone close, such as a friend or relative.

"Well, as we were waiting, at a respectable distance, I noticed another body laid out for examination. I recognised him straightaway. It was our dismembering murder suspect! It transpired he had held a nurse hostage in the prison pharmacy, helped himself to a load of prescription pills and various drugs, and promptly OD'd[19] as a result!"

A neat irony, no doubt. But now the Box was closed and the lid firmly locked down again. DeVille was once more telling the tale he chose to tell, in the way he chose to tell it. I looked around and saw that the other listeners had finished their drinks and were beginning to gather their things together. It was getting late and it was time to leave.

---

[19] i.e. taken an over-dose (Ed.)

A Bad Business in Brighton

It was a splendid dinner. The Lord Mayor had presented his awards for charitable work, to a variety of worthy winners, with the minimum of fuss and no lengthy speeches. A thoroughly professional job. And I had not had to wear black-tie which, as some may know, is against my beliefs, but needs must.

After we had finished the last course and the port and brandy had been served, the Mayor introduced us to his after-dinner speaker, none other than DeVille himself. I was totally surprised – caught completely off-guard, in fact. He had not let slip that he would be speaking at this event. I knew he was planning to do some public speaking but had thought he would commence his career in more intimate and less grand circumstances. I was mistaken.

He begins:

"Thank you, Lord Mayor."

He pauses – looking around at the diverse members of his audience, assessing their degree of interest, their appearance and demeanour, for each of these aspects is equally discernible to the trained eye of our detective, connoisseur of human nature.

"This evening I would like to invite you to examine with me the narrative of violent behaviour. You will all be aware that the Mayor's initiatives against violent crime in our City – the VRU (Violent Response Unit) and the CHP (Community Health Programme) – have started to take effect. Hopefully they will prove successful. But I wish to tell a cautionary tale to temper what may otherwise be unrealistic expectations. It is a tale of woe. It is a tale of modern violence and the social ills of our time. If you are sitting comfortably – at least for the moment – then let us begin:

One summer, a few years ago, I was seconded to the local Force down in Sussex, based in Brighton, as it happened. I was there specifically to assist with investigating cases of murder. I was tasked with training some of the local officers in this area of expertise. However, I sometimes became involved in other cases, to a greater or lesser extent. One of these began as an instance of *routine* domestic violence but soon escalated into something far more serious. One afternoon we were called to a boarding house near the sea-front. Out of season these B&Bs are usually sleepy establishments but sometimes they will have *Housing Benefit* claimants. In season you never know, from one week to the next, who will be in residence. On this occasion, however, the lodgers had been housed by the local council and had been there for the last couple of months. When we arrived they could be heard shouting and swearing in the upstairs rooms– a real *ding-dong* affair! The ferocious barking of a dog accompanied the rumpus and a baby was howling with all the unlikely power of its little lungs. Constable Roberts knocked firmly on the door – a momentary silence ... As the door suddenly banged open an aluminium saucepan came flying past the constable's head and hit the first and largest of three plaster ducks hanging on the wall behind us, smashing it to smithereens! Then a slavering set of teeth, surrounded by the face of an enormous bull-like terrier, launched from the doorway and was halted only inches from my knee by a fierce tug on its harness, causing it to fly upwards into the air as if hauled back by an invisible tractor beam. This was our introduction to the Puginello family.

On the occasion of our next visit, at the invitation of Social Care, who were concerned in particular for the baby's welfare, we met with two black eyes: one his and one hers. She held a rolling pin in one hand and a bottle of gin in the other; he held a gnarled walking-stick and a copy of the *Racing Times*. Odds-on this was a domestic dispute provoked by one of the common vices of either drinking or gambling, or possibly both. We found the baby playing happily with the bull-terrier, tickling its tummy as it lay on its back. As soon as it saw us the dog sat up and snarled aggressively. Mr Puginello pulled it away and shut the dog in the next-door room. For this we were grateful.

I should mention, at this point that, today, under the Dangerous Dogs Act, such a creature would not be permitted as a pet. Indeed, our local colleagues informed us that Puginello had a bit of history when it came to housing wild animals. In the past these had included: piranhas, feral ferrets, and even a small crocodile which was kept in the bath. The baby, however, appeared to be well cared for, with no obvious signs of injury or neglect. The Social Worker was satisfied, for the time being, that the family, though it had problems, was not an especial cause for concern. Unfortunately, this assessment proved to be quite mistaken.

A few days later Constable Roberts arrived at the station sporting a black eye, limping a bit, and with his arm in plaster.

'Blimey lad, you've been in the wars! What's happened to you?'

'It's the Puginellos. Mrs P. was chasing Mr P. down the street, holding the baby under one arm and thumping him with her shopping bag, which she held in the other hand. There were eggs and beer cans and butcher's sausages sent spinning in all directions!

'Didn't you try and stop him?'

'What? No. I couldn't. He knocked me over. As I got up again Mrs P. ran into me and sent me flying as she chased after him. And *then* I was bitten by the bloomin' dog, which picked up the string of sausages and ran off with them trailing behind!'

He rolled up his right trouser leg to reveal a large bruise but no broken skin. A lucky case of the bark being worse than the bite, I thought. Apparently, Mr P. had been tasked with looking after the child while his wife went out for some shopping. When she returned the baby was in a pushchair on the pavement right by the edge of the road and Mr P. was nowhere to be seen. Just then he came around the corner with a copy of the Racing Times in his hands, eagerly studying the form. And hence the *mariticidal* pursuit, the *inuxorious* escape, and the *unfortunate*, though not life-threatening, injuries to Constable Roberts.

And, I might add, this sort of scene was being rehearsed and performed all over the country, especially in coastal towns. Something about the sea air and the hot summer sun, I suppose. Who knows?

Anyway, it must have been the following weekend, early evening I think. We got a call to go and sort out a bit of a brawl down at the old *Cock & Bull*. By the time we arrived two constables had been flattened, one out cold, and three others were only just managing to restrain Puginello. We waded in, as necessary.

Breach of the Peace. Magistrates Court. Usual fine. Bound Over. Standard procedure. Ineffective.

There followed a litany of cautionary offences: beating up the publican of the *Railway Tavern*; threatening behaviour towards the local Member of Parliament; allowing a dangerous dog off the leash in a public space; defacing the recently restored Brighton Pavilion with a Banksy-style mural[20]; and, lastly, a charge of urinating in public. But this was small beer. Last Thursday he murdered his wife. Her body was found on the steep shingle beach just to the west of Brighton Pier. He left the baby, sleeping in its cot, but took the dog.

Puginello was seen getting off a slam-door train at platform 5, Victoria Station, London – before the train had completely stopped. There were several eye-witnesses, including an itinerant jazz pianist on the main concourse. Puginello was shouting something about a crocodile as he dashed along the platform and down into the Underground. He was pursued by the dog. We finally caught up with him just opposite Paddington Station, at an Italian *Gelateria*, which offered the best ice-cream in all London. He was quite placid and happily feasting on *frutta di bosca*. The dog was licking its *pistachio* and its lips.

Shortly thereafter Puginello was sentenced to indefinite confinement at *Long Heath*, a secure hospital for the criminally insane. It was located far inland and at the greatest possible distance from the sea. Here he received few visitors but the best care possible in every way. I went to see him once, but he made no sense at all. The only words he ever said, and kept repeating, as if some refrain from a once popular music hall song, or perhaps a once well-known pantomime, were:

"That's the way to do it! That's the way to do it!"

---

[20] It later transpired that this was actually a Banksy mural of considerable worth, but by then the local council had removed it.

Cards, Capers and Collections

It is raining. It has been raining all day. I doubt it will stop raining. The cards that drop onto the doormat each day suggest scenes of snow, deep and crisp and even. It may be so in the far north, among the reindeer or the caribou, but here it is raining. There is still a whole week to go till Christmas Day. More rain is forecast. But let's not allow that to put a dampener on things!

DeVille agrees. I ask him about Christmas at the Police Station, back in the early days. Not just at the Station, he says. And not just us Coppers neither! I ask him to explain, to expand upon this extravagant claim. He needs no further invitation and is out of the trap like – well, I can't say a greyhound, perhaps more like a distracted spaniel that goes this way, then that, following old trails and trials, picking up new scents and smells and generally leading us all in a round and round about merry dance to one unexpected place or, as often as not, another, just as unlikely.

On this occasion we are asked to picture DeVille enjoying a quiet pint alone in a nearby pub. He is neither quietly contemplative nor unduly alert. He is simply enjoying a drink at the bar within sight of Old Father Thames and within the sound of Bow Bells. On that particular afternoon he has given evidence at the Old Bailey and is now relaxing before he makes his way home for the evening. Tomorrow he is on the early relief.

I was approached by a man – in his early thirties, I'd say. He had been sitting over by the window, casting the odd glance in my direction. I recognised him. After a few minutes he came over to the bar and ordered another drink. Then he turned to me and said:

"I hope you don't mind me asking, but don't I know you?"

"I should think so," said DeVille, "I put you away for that Mile End burglary!"

"Blimey! It's you – well I'll be damned! Let me buy you a drink. I can't thank you enough for what you did. Saw the error of

89

my ways after that. Stopped all that thieving malarkey for good after that. Got a job with the GPO. Doing computers nowadays. Still with the wife and we're very happy. Haven't let her down once since then. All thanks to you – never had a chance to say thank you till now!"

DeVille graciously accepted the offer of a drink, allowing his glass to be refilled with best London bitter.

"So, are you still stationed down at Holborn then?"

"Not any more, no," answered DeVille, "I'm with Scotland Yard now."

After chatting for a while DeVille made his excuses and left. But that was not the last of it. That Christmas, and every Christmas thereafter, DeVille received a card from this grateful ex-con. As a matter of fact, this was not as exceptional as it sounds. DeVille continues to receive a variety of cards at Christmas, both from within the U.K. and from abroad, still religiously forwarded from the sorting office at Scotland Yard. Many are from ex-colleagues and friends but there is also a fair smattering of cards from the Costa del Sol and even a few from Down Under. DeVille is also reputed to have shares in *Rio Tinto* but I think that is rather far-fetched. However, while some rumours are merely mischievous, others are downright libellous. This is perhaps one such but I have it on good authority, DeVille's to be precise, that it is true.

DeVille continued:

"Over the Christmas period there were very few people about and there was very little happening in the heart of the Capital, in the City of London itself. Nothing moved: not a beer-wagon, not a butcher's van, even the famous black-cabs were absent. All seemed still and unnaturally quiet. It was like a ghost town. The only hint of a sound was the creaking by the jetty of what must have been Old Marley's chains or the cry of the unknown jumper who flew off Blackfriar's Bridge those many years ago and whose body was never found.

But we liked to uphold a longstanding Christmas tradition – unwritten and unacknowledged, naturally – but a tradition nonetheless. It involved all of us *Peelers* here in the City of London. This included the Police Stations at: Snow Hill, Holborn Circus, Old Bailey, the Meat Market and maybe one or two others. Part of this tradition was that various appreciative

Publicans would drop off, at each respective Station, a case of light ales, the odd bottle of Scotch (no wine in them days, of course), and a few bottles of Tizer for the (very) few tea-totallers among the local bobbies. The unspoken rule was that if you worked Christmas Day or Boxing Day as a driver, you worked only the one and would not be driving the next – so you could have a drink! The combination of inactivity in the City and the festive atmosphere engendered by crates of ale, encouraged a bit of competition between the various local Nicks. It was par for the course to lift a Panda car's wheel from the opposition and issue a ransom for the same wheel!

I remember one year when I was doing a split-shift as usual. Now there were not many WPCs in them days, you know. There was just the one in Holborn then. She was out on patrol. She hadn't checked in on the half hour as expected so we called her up on radio:

"505, 505" from Echo Oscar – please specify your current location?' (Noise of static …)

Just then we received a call on the old Dolls-Eye switchboard. We had recently moved into a modern 1968 office but were still in the process of upgrading to the new comms system. Saunders took the call and put it on speaker:

'Are you by any chance looking for WPC 505? It's going to cost you two cases of light ale. To be delivered to the usual drop off point.'

She'd been kidnapped by City of London Police – the Snow Hill Mob!

The Duty Sarge spoke up:

'Right you two – we need to sort out something here! We've only got four cases. Two cases to get her back?'

'Well, do we really need her back?' asked Saunders.

'When she starts complaining they'll soon release her!

Let's scam it and put one full case on top of an empty one!' I said.

So that's exactly what we did.

About twenty minutes later Snow Hill called again. Saunders picked up the handset:

'We think you're giving us the run around,' Snow Hill said.

'Would we do such a thing?', Saunders replied, trying but failing to keep a straight face.

'Nah! You're not keeping to the bargain – now we want some lager too!'

We'd been rumbled!

The Sarge was insistent – we needed to get WPC 505 back. There followed a lengthy period of intricate bartering and delicate negotiation, with a little liquid lubrication to aid the vocalisation of terms and conditions.

I suggested we leave WPC 505 there, where she was, till end of the shift. Of course, we didn't know it then, but she was partying away like billy-o with the Snow Hill Mob. One of her mates, another WPC, was based over there, I believe. Anyway WPC 505 eventually cost us another two cases of Light Ale. When we did the exchange at 'Checkpoint Charlie' it was like something out of a Cold War thriller:

"Why did you rescue me so soon? I was enjoying myself!" said WPC 505, a bit too loudly.

Rather than take her back to the Station at Holborn we thought it best to call a *lifeboat*[21] to drop her back at her flat and let her sleep it off.

The next day we did some infiltration of our own. Passing unseen over no-man's land, we soon found the opposition's Panda and helped ourselves to a couple of nearside wheels. Now they would be going nowhere fast. We beat a discrete retreat, rolling the wheels back over the bridge that divided our *Manors*. Needless to say, they finally got their wheels back just as soon as we got all our Light Ales back – well those they hadn't already demolished – and a bottle of scotch as a bonus. Now we were quits. At the end of the day, after a final parley, we all got together for drinks over at Snow Hill. WPC 505, however, did not reappear in time for this combined performance!"

DeVille was now in full flight. Before one story had ended another began:

---

[21] See *The Columbo of Kensington* (Ed.)

"Did I ever tell you about the incident up at Notting Hill? This was back in the 1980s. I was having a drink with a couple of buddies after work. We'd been on a training course together and fancied a drink before getting down to an evening's homework. Anyway, in those days the regulations governing charity collections meant that you were not allowed to collect donations in an open vessel; the collection box must be sealed and un-interferable with. Additionally, the collector needed to have ID, permission from the Police, and a document specifying the details of the charity concerned."

As they were talking together DeVille noticed someone enter the Saloon Bar with an open charity box. He said he was collecting for the Miners. Must have been back in the mid 80s sometime. DeVille's radar was alerted. Something not quite right here – no, he's dodgy!

Just then he saw the collector twist the box over and put the donations into a bag. He then gave it to his mate, who immediately stuffed it into his pocket. DeVille leapt up and grabbed the collector, holding him in a secure armlock. His accomplice ran off.

"Ere, what you doin'? Who do you think you are?"

"Don't you recognise me? I'm The Old Bill," says DeVille.

The collector's face dropped and his shoulders slumped. How would DeVille deal with him? Always keen that justice should be served, he bypassed the paperwork that would have been required if he had hauled him off to the Nick. Instead DeVille took him to a nearby Pub, The Red Lion. Now this incident happened in the days before all-day opening, so different drinking establishments would keep different opening hours.

The Governor at the Red Lion just happened to be a fellow Rotary member and just happened to have six different collection boxes lined up along the bar, from RNLI to Guide Dogs, from Seamans' Mission to the Children's Hospice, and a couple of other local charities.

'Right, show the landlord your collection box – and show him how it works? Show him how you open it?'

'Open it? I can't open it!'

'Oh yes you can!'

'Oh no I can't!'

DeVille took the collection box and gave it a twist. Then he handed it back.

"*Now see these six different collection boxes? They all need filling up.*"

Begrudgingly each box was filled, filled to the brim, in a miracle to rival that of the Loaves & Fishes. When the collecting box was at last empty he asked:

"*Can I have my box back now?*"

"*Here you are,*" said Deville, "*but you'll need dustpan & brush mate. Now stamp on it or I'll stamp on you!*"

And then there was that occasion over in South Croydon, down at the *Barrow & Plough*, sometime in the early '90s, I think it was. There were eight of us CID officers. It was a couple of weeks before Christmas and the pub was decked with old-fashioned non-flashing lights and coloured chain-loops – you know, the ones we used to make as kids? We decided we'd join in with the carol singers and were half way through '*While Shepherds Watched*' to the tune of *Ilkley Moor Bar tat* – when a woman came in, about thirty, I'd say, reasonably well-dressed, and wearing a ring on her left hand. She said she was collecting for the Children's Hospital at St. Swithins. Well, I'd not heard of this particular establishment, as it happened. But my mates thought I was just being an old Scrooge – '*Oh come on DeVille, cough up – put a fiver in!*' they cried. But I wasn't going to be put off and I asked to see her *bona fides*, her letter of Authority. She produced a document but the name had been typexed out and another name, her own as it happened, inserted instead.

"*Where are you from then?*" I asked.

She said she was from Thamesmead. Now I thought to myself: that's South-East London, near Belmarsh.

"*So who's looking after your kids then – a neighbour?*"

"*I ain't got no kids*", she said.

"*Come on, leave it DeVille!*" the lads cried. But I was not going to let it go.

"*How do you get around? Where's your driver?*" I asked.

So we went outside and discovered the Son of Pearly King, seated in an old six litre Jaguar. So we go up to him and I ask if he has any more collection boxes. He opens the boot for me and, blow me, there's a dozen boxes and six of them are jam-packed full. Not looking good here. This time I took them straight down the Nick.

Enquiries revealed that this particular Pearly Prince was collecting lots of money for the hospital. The Bursar said he gave her about £120 a month for the last 12-18 months but it had recently risen to nearer £200 a month. She also confirmed he had twenty collection boxes in his possession, together with more than 500 sealing rings.

It just so happened the six boxes we are holding down at the Nick have a total of £1000 in them. And that was just the collection for that one evening.

"But he seemed such a nice bloke!" the Bursar said.

I reckon he must have been making up to £5000 a week.

Anyway, two or three months later I called The Bursar. I explained that she had previously been breaking the law by not following the correct procedure for charitable collections. However, I would not take the matter any further. Then a few months later still I received a call from her. They were now doing collections directly and the sums raised were now in the order of £4000 a month.'

Looking around I said that I thought the weather might be brightening up now.

"Still raining though, aint it?" said DeVille. Just then his cab arrived and he tumbled in. I finished my drink, checked my phone for messages, then made a dash for the train station over the road, dodging the large puddles as best I could. Taking off my hat and shaking off the worst of the rain, I noticed a group of carol singers on the concourse and as I put my ticket into the machine to open the barrier they started singing *Hosanna in Excelsis!* The chorus of voices trembled tunefully, like a peal of Christmas bells and, for a moment, I thought I heard a familiar mellow tenor among all the other voices.

Curlers

I once stopped off loch-side in the Cairngorms to watch a curling team practising their arcane and historic sport. Nowadays curling is deemed worthy of the Olympics but, back in the day, it was merely a pleasant past-time. Apparently the majority of stones are themselves hewn from the granite rocks of Ailsa Craig, a volcanic island at the southern end of the Firth of Clyde. But I digress.

We were seated once more at the *Pig & Whistle*. By the time I arrived DeVille had already begun to draw a small crowd. I ordered a drink and then took my place in the audience and settled down to enjoy the performance. I have mentioned elsewhere DeVille's skill as an observer and his ability to deduce things from the seemingly most insignificant detail. In the following story DeVille relates how this came as naturally to him as breathing. He was off duty and out of uniform. It was his day off. Not that he was ever *off-duty*. In fact he was more often skiing *off-piste* than ever he was off-duty. His unorthodox approach, based on keen observation and a gifted insight into human nature, meant that he would often take an unusual step, or pursue a seemingly unlikely lead, that others would never have noticed or considered. More often than not he was proven right in his interpretation. This is one such story, in which suspicion is the precursor of proof.

"Now we used to use the old *Twelve-A Book*. The *Twelve-A Book* was a large desk book where everything was completed in copper-plate hand-writing. There was no allowance for crossings-out. It was about eighteen inches tall by fifteen inches wide. Don't ask me for centimetres. It had a green spine, extending about two to three inches on to the cover, and was one of a series of books, known by their number, that every station possessed. Basically it was a gospel record of every collar we'd made, of every incident reported, of every person of possible interest. The motto we applied was: '*Catch'em, Book'em, Charge'em*'. If you did the first then you had to complete the next stage, and the next – there was no leaving things half-done. Call it

'Principles of Policing', if you like – there were several, some written down in formal procedures, and others very much part of an unwritten code and culture. However, if there was insufficient evidence to proceed to a charge, then an entry was made in the *Twelve-A* tome. That way everything was clearly recorded, in case a charge was made subsequently, or if an investigation was carried out by internal affairs for some dubious reason. It could prove an invaluable source of evidence to exonerate the officers on duty at the time, proving they had acted correctly."

I listened intently, supping at my pint, not sure if I had heard this tale – or elements of it – previously. DeVille's stories seemed to interweave themselves and travel in a variety of unlikely directions. He continued:

"I was on my way home one evening, driving back from visiting my great aunt over Watford way. I had a lovely old *Morris Traveller* back then, god bless her. Long gone now. Beautiful woodwork and an engine that purred like a Cheshire cat. Of course, in those days it was perfectly possible to drive through central London without any bother, especially on a Sunday. Anyway, I must have been passing near Oxford Street; I was heading for Waterloo Bridge. I saw a bloke hop out of a taxi; he was about forty, totally bald – or his head was shaved maybe – and carrying a large blue suitcase. The odd thing was that, as soon as the taxi had done a U-turn and headed across the road to pick up another fare, this bloke proceeds to hold up his thumb and starts to hitch a lift. Naturally, I stopped and asked him where he was headed. Luckily I was going in the very same direction and he hopped in, placing his suitcase on the back seat and getting in to the front passenger's seat. So we got chatting, as you do, and he told me he could let me have a set of hair-curlers, brand-new, for a fiver. Now I happened to know that *new* they were at least thirty quid as I'd just bought some for my Aunt, at her request (she wanted to reimburse me but I wouldn't let her – 'an early Christmas present', I told her). Anyways, as I was saying, this bald bloke offers these curlers to me for just five quid. I had a hunch. No evidence, as such, just an informed *hunch*, as you might say. So we drove on till we reached our destination – well, my destination, which seemed to be the right place for the both of us. Through an archway, into a courtyard, and behind some mews flats, we arrived at Holborn Police Station, back entrance.

My lift enquired about the Panda Cars parked in the yard, and the large Black Van with grilled windows. *'Blimey, you're not the Old Bill, are ya?'* Yes, I assured him, the very same – and you're nicked mate!"

At that point we halted, momentarily, while more drinks arrived and were generously distributed by Julian, who had joined us after work. His office is just over the road. We gentlemen of leisure, meanwhile, had already downed our initial drinks and were pleased to see him. I explained we were talking about *curlers* and he immediately recalled the story – or some of it – but not the ending. We settled again and DeVille continued:

"Right, so I had this guy on suspicion of possessing stolen property and trying to fence it off. So I took him into the station, to the main desk. There I found two desk sergeants on duty – it was a typically busy Sunday night and nothing much at all was happening. Now you need to understand that it was a couple of years since I'd been based in Holborn, so I didn't know these two clowns. And they didn't know me either. They were not inclined to complete the booking forms for my collar. They suggested I had no substantial evidence for my charge. I was not having that. There are times when you need to pull rank, make use of your contacts, see justice done – this was one of them. I called my old D.I. It was one o'clock in the morning. He wasn't too pleased to be disturbed but I explained the situation and he backed me up. I put him on speaker to the two sergeant-clowns: They were to keep the suspect confined till morning when the D.I. would himself, personally, arrive to confirm the arrest. 'Nuff said."

"So what happened the next morning?" I asked.

"Well, the D.I. was as good as his word. Not only that, but the daily district teletext had provided an update on all local incidents occurring within the last twenty-four hours. And what do you know? It reported a theft of electrical goods, specifically fifty boxes of curlers, from a shop in Oxford Street, matching the description of those found on the person of our would be *hitch-hiker.*"

"So the D.I. did turn up the next morning!"

"He certainly did. Gave them two Jokers a right official *pollocking!*"

However, he was vindicated when his suspect, *Curley Jones*, pleaded guilty to burglary and was given an eighteen month custodial holiday, courtesy of the Crown Court. There followed a Judge's commendation and, eventually, a Commissioner's commendation also, something not often awarded except for exceptional dedication or, as in DeVille's case, obsessive devotion to justice and the law. After each ceremony, as tradition dictates, the recipient, DeVille on these occasions, bought drinks all round. Unfortunately I missed both of these unlikely opportunities.

"But that wasn't the end of it", said DeVille. "Some time later one of them Jokers approached me after a seminar down at the Police College in Henley – now what was it about? – well it doesn't matter, but he sought me out and challenged me:

'What do you think you were doing, going over our heads like that? Why did you call the D.I. about the arrest? Don't you think that was a bit out of order?' he said.

'Not at all', I replied. 'Look, it's just the two of us here now, right? There's nobody else. So let me tell you how it is. You don't piss off your colleagues in CID like you did, refusing to register an arrest just to avoid the paperwork, right? Let me tell you, if I ever come across you and your fellow-Joker again – and you give me or anyone else the run around – I will personally see to it that the rest of your career is spent in Traffic Control. *Comprendez*?'

I sat and smiled wryly. Julian was highly amused and laughed with undiluted delight. Harvey, who had slipped into the circle almost unnoticed, looked at each of us and followed suit. DeVille sat back with a look of sublime satisfaction upon his face as he drew on his cigar and contemplated the new bottle of *Pinot Grigio* that had just been placed in front of him, courtesy of the landlord.

Apparently he found out, sometime later, that our two *Jokers* had left the police force and formed their own private investigation agency, called *Barnums,* I believe. It was based down on the south coast somewhere near Bognor Regis. That venture didn't last very long; the last DeVille heard was that they were performing at the end of the pier and on Mediterranean cruise ships, where no paperwork was ever needed. Unfortunately none of this is actually recorded in the *Twelve-A Book* so I cannot be sure of its accuracy!

As we left the *Pig & Whistle* I turned to thank the landlord for hosting our gathering. As I did so I noticed an old black and white photograph, that I had not seen before, hanging high on the wall behind the bar. It showed a young Olympic medal-winning team. They posed together in front of the *Jungfrau*, holding long-handled brushes, with their dark-grey curling stones laid out before them on the smooth ice. One of the team looked strangely familiar, but I couldn't quite place him. I was about to ask the landlord about the photograph when DeVille declared his taxi had just arrived – he must be off! That was our cue and we each left to go our separate ways. I had forgotten all about the photograph until just now.

Colwyn Bay Calling

I was about to ask DeVille how he had acquired his rather unusual nickname when he suddenly said:

"Did I ever tell you about the big favour we did for the Welsh boys?"

"I'm not sure. Tell me anyway," I said, giving him the unnecessary licence to continue. DeVille began to recount his story as we sat at a table in the *Pig and Whistle* supping our pints. The muzak and the hubbub of other conversations receded into the background as he conjured his tale into existence.

It is six p.m. on a Sunday evening, DeVille and Saunders are, once again, working together on the graveyard shift. However, unlike Burke and Hare, they are not seeking to provide fresh bodies to medical students for dissection. They are instead catching up on the paperwork for the *bodies*[22] they had dealt with during that week.

Deville receives a call from Colwyn Bay. It was the North Wales Police asking for help on one of their more serious cases.

"Is that Scotland Yard then?"

"No, it's Albany Street, CID, nearly Scotland Yard. Detective Deville speaking. How can we be of assistance?"

He puts the call on speakerphone so Saunders can listen in. Saunders looks up briefly and indicates he is all ears. He is also polishing his shoes, he is polishing them so well that he can see not only his own face in them, but also the shape of his mother's eyes in his own. DeVille was generally less particular about his footwear. His blackened boots were worn at heel and needed a visit to the cobbler. DeVille made a mental note.

"Well, it's like this, see? We've had a murder and we believe the suspect has made their way to London," said D.S. (Detective Superintendent) Jones from Colwyn Bay.

"I see, so how can we help?"

"Well, they would have arrived at Euston yesterday afternoon,

---

[22] Police colloquial term meaning prisoner/s

about five-thirty. We were hoping you could check out the hotels in the area to trace and arrest them. Can you do that for us, boy'o? I'll give you a description of the main suspect and her accomplices. You see the suspect has got her young son with her, you know, and her dog too. Don't suppose that's much to go on but thought you'd better have all the information, like."

DeVille took down the details:

1. Female (*name redacted*), white, 35 years old, 5'8", slim build, brown hair
2. Male (*name redacted),* white, 5 years old, 3'1", sleight build, brown hair
3. Dog (*Snowdon*), collie cross-breed, speaks Welsh

"We'll do our best, but there are quite a large number of hotels and B&Bs near Euston Station and the surrounding areas," DeVille replied.

"Well, do the best you can then, won't you now? I'm counting on you."

"Yes Sir, of course," said DeVille.

DeVille put the phone down and proceeded to consider the number of hotels and B&Bs in the vicinity of Euston – probably one or two hundred more than are to be found on the seafront in Colwyn Bay – and he wondered. He wondered at the possibility of finding the suspects, in flight from Colwyn Bay. He wondered at the assumption that such a search could be conducted with the limited resources at his disposal i.e. only Saunders and himself. And, just for a moment, he wondered what had induced him to join the Police Force in the first place. DeVille caught himself thinking like this and, pushing the chair away from the desk, stood up briskly. There were a lot of doors to knock on and a lot of numbers to call. This was going to be a difficult and painstaking enquiry. Best get on with it.

Saunders' zen-like attention to his shoes came to a sudden end as DeVille *accidentally* stepped on his foot. That did the trick. Saunders started showing a little bit more interest and, incidentally, needed to do a bit more polishing on one shoe in particular. Suddenly Deville shouted '*Eureka!*' like some modern-day Archimedes and exclaimed:

"Miracles, miracles, miracles on a Sunday graveyard shift! Saunders, it's going to be a long night. We might have to call in some troops, which you will do, as I am not waking up detectives in the early hours, that's your job."

Saunders grimaced.

"Come on Saunders, we've work to do. I've got an idea. This is how we'll go about things."

Deville then proceeded to explain his strategy. The train route began at Colywn Bay, passed through Chester and eventually arrived at London Euston. Deville reminded Saunders that Euston station had been rebuilt and, at that time, a state of the art CCTV system had been installed. This might be useful.

"We need to enlist the help of our colleagues in the British Transport Police. They are the experts."

Saunders felt relieved. He would not, after all, need to wake up colleagues from their well-earned slumbers and he would not, after all, be getting an earful for his pains. Instead they made their way to London Euston railway station, which was only about 5 minutes from the Albany Street Police Station. They went to the British Transport Police office and, as luck would have it, there was a detective on duty who Deville knew very well and had worked with on many occasions in the past. He was Scottish and was affectionately known as The *Flying Scotsman*. Deville was not sure whether this nickname, this apposite Scottish soubriquet, came from the speed at which the detective arrested suspects or the speed at which he could down a *wee dram* or two. Possibly both. Be that as it may, together they reviewed the CCTV footage from the previous evening and, low and behold, the suspect, her little boy, and the sheep dog Snowdon, were seen going down to the lower level of the station where the Black Cabs[23] pick up fares. Detective *Flying Scotsman* suggested they put a notice board up near the taxi rank asking if any taxi driver had picked up a middle-aged female, a small boy and a Welsh speaking sheep dog the day before.

They were in luck! After a short period of chatting with the cabbies at the rank, to see if any of them remembered a woman with a child and a Welsh dog, the sixth cabbie – or maybe the

---

[23] Traditional London taxis

seventh, I'm not sure – said he thought he remembered them. He had dropped them off in Argyle Square the evening before, at a B&B that allowed dogs, especially Welsh speaking dogs, as the owner was Welsh herself.

Deville turned to Saunders and said:

"Which method of detection are we going to use? *Miracle* or *Eureka*?"

Saunders grimaced for only the second time that evening.

"No more grimacing. This is proper detective work!" declared DeVille.

The Cabbie, Tom, who had taken the suspects to Argyle Square agreed to take Deville and Saunders to the same place, but not before explaining to the cabbies in front, on the rank, that he was assisting police detectives in an enquiry, and not in fact queue jumping.

Tom the Cab turned off his meter and took Deville and Saunders to *The Black Swan* in Argyle Square. It was an old pub, long since converted into a B&B, suitable for casual travellers and tourists alike. As they got out of the taxi Tom turned and said:

'Watch out for that dog of theirs. Very bright them Collies. Bit of Alsatian in him too, I'd say. I reckon he knows more than he lets on. He seems to understand English as well as Welsh. When I handed them their luggage and said goodbye he came up to me and put out his paw to shake my hand.'

'We'll bear that in mind,' said Saunders. DeVille continued:

"I spoke to the man on reception, a Greek Cypriot chap, been over here since the war, married a Welsh girl. He gave us a master key and directed us to a room at the end of the corridor up on the second floor."

'But shouldn't we wait for backup?' Saunders asked rather sensibly. 'I mean, they are wanted for suspected murder. They could be dangerous, possibly even armed and who knows how much English the dog understands.'

"What backup would that be?"

They didn't have any backup available. Deville suggested that Saunders (ex-military) call in the SAS (Saunders grimaced once more) but he said they were already busy abseiling elsewhere in London at some unspecified foreign Embassy. So instead they knocked on the door.

DeVille had taken the Colwyn Bay call at 18:22 that evening. By 21:45 Deville and Saunders had taken into custody the suspect, her boy and Snowdon, the by now bilingual Border Collie-cross!

D. S. Jones of Colwyn Bay was very pleased and couldn't believe the speed at which Deville and Saunders obtained a result. He sent an escort to collect their 'package' the very next day.

Snowdon, the dog, wasn't read his rights and later got off on a technicality. He couldn't be taken back to the mountain he was named after, so DeVille looked after him for a few days until he was adopted by a family via the Battersea Dogs Home. It was his work on this case that originally earned Detective Deville the curious soubriquet of *The Urban Shepherd.*

The best result was that the Welsh colleagues from Colwyn Bay brought Deville and Saunders a thank you gift: two bottles of Welsh malt whiskey. Deville and Saunders were surprised, as they thought they were all teetotal in that part of the world. Clearly, they were mistaken. They were hoping to enjoy an unexpected reward for a job well done. Unfortunately, the Chief Superintendent had already been contacted by D. S. Jones from North Wales.

"I have sent my officers to collect the prisoners and escort them back to North Wales. My officers will leave a gift of gratitude to your outstanding officers, Deville and Saunders, who greatly helped us on this case."

The tradition at this time was that the Chief Superintendent (the *Governor*), would be included in any *thank you*. As a matter of fact the Governor was Welsh himself and bilingual. One bottle of Welsh Malt duly landed on his desk.

Sometimes a strange telephone call, an unusual request, results in a *Miracle*. For the North Wales officers, it was a miracle. For Deville and Saunders, on another graveyard shift, it was a 'result' and they toasted it together. Later in the week they finished the bottle of Welsh malt whiskey, just between themselves, as they worked on another gruelling graveyard shift.

And so it was that, without actually asking, I finally discovered how DeVille came by his unusual nickname.

The Grand Piano

It is known worldwide that anything and everything is available at *Harrods* and may be readily purchased, even if at a quite unreasonable price. Whilst *John Lewis* may never knowingly be undersold, they will not supply many of the obscure, original, and ethnographic items to be found in the avenues and halls, the marinas and canals, the dry-docks and harbours, of the archetypal super store that is *Harrods*.

Tonight DeVille reminded me of a story I had once heard him tell, though it had escaped my recollection until his casual remark. It was about a Grand Piano that stood on display in the Main Foyer at *Harrods*. She was a *Steinway*, of the very best quality and craftsmanship, most refined and elegant. She was aesthetically akin to a *Stradivarius*. Made from North West Pacific rock-maple, She was polished and tuned to perfection and merely awaited a brilliant pianist to bring her to life.

The Grand Piano waits expectantly, like a great ocean liner at her privileged moorings, aware of her own magnificence and importance. She is impatient to be purchased and to be played. She imagines her Virtuoso performing at the Royal Albert Hall to an audience in awe of her effortless power and delicate tone. His fingers stroke and caress her ivory and ebony keys with the sensitive touch of extensive and refined musical experience. She feels the thunder of her own bass notes tremble through her feet and travel across the stage, out into the surrounding streets, and beyond. She feels the lightest touches tingle as her high notes wing across the air and rise like lanterns into the night. But tonight, as the bell tolls and the last stewards leave the *S.S. Harrods*, before the nightguard begins his rounds, tonight all is silent. *As silent as a painted ship ...*

One day not long after, as the Grand Piano was comparing her own shapely legs to those of the very rich ladies shopping for lipstick and perfumes nearby, She was unexpectedly disturbed from the vanity of her reverie. She caught sight of a group of four men, all dressed in the standard brown overall of the Delivery

Department. Their leader asked for directions at the *Caisse* and then She saw the cashier point in her direction. She looked around: there was nothing behind her, nothing to the left of her, and nothing to the right of her – apart from a large floral display and some small Ottomans, nothing that required the combined might of four men from the Stores Department. They approached indirectly, tacking between *Exotic Fruits* and *Desert Cacti*. As they hove closer, she suddenly felt both nervous and excited, all at the same time. Her feet began to tingle and her hammers started to flutter, her pedals twitched, and she felt her strings vibrate in anticipated fifths.

"Right lads, secure the sounding-board!" cried the Captain. And so they did. And they battened down the pedals and shuttered off the keyboard too. And then the captain ordered his crew to weigh anchor and loose the mainsail. Slowly the Grand Piano began to move with a leeward wind, as gently She headed from harbour out towards the open sea.

In those days there was no CCTV, of course. Technology had not yet insinuated itself into each and every corner, every crevice, of every department store and every city street. There was no cinematic record, no visible evidence, no taping of the present that must inevitably become the past, no record of the *moment* of criminal action. And that was why it was possible. Or, at least, that was why it took some time to discover both the fact and the consequences of the fact; that is why it took some considerable time before an act of piracy was detected.

The next morning DeVille got a call from a store detective, Gerald, a buddy of his from the old Holborn days, now retired from the Met. and supplementing his pinch of a pension with some light duties over in Knightsbridge. DeVille takes up the story:

"Calm down Gerald. What's the problem exactly? A piano, yes? A *Grand* Piano – I see. And when was this exactly? Yesterday afternoon. And you noticed this when? This morning. Eleven o'clock. I see."

I raised an eyebrow? DeVille paused to light his cigar, enjoying the moment of revelation, and then he continued:

"Okay, we'll be straight over and you can fill us in on the details."

DeVille told us how they motored over to South Kensington and parked their Panda car in the Chairman's bay. Fortunately he was away in Paris at the time. A few more details and a few notes taken, it soon became evident that the Grand Piano had gone walkabout, though it was by no means certain as to where – it may as well have been Walsingham or Woomera! With no CCTV monitor in place, witnesses were interviewed. It all took time. In the end a van was identified: *O'Malley and Sons, Removals & Storage. 46, High St. Ealing.*

DeVille's attention was distracted by the arrival of new additions to his audience. Julian and Harvey had been in on it from the beginning but now Jane and Jennifer arrived, armed with a fresh bottle of dry white wine. I had not met either before and it was only later that I realised neither had DeVille. Nevertheless they accepted his invitation to join the party and soon were inevitably charmed, captivated, and held unwitting prisoners in equal measure. By the time I picked up the main narrative again, we have moved on. Once more DeVille takes up the story:

"Now the funny thing was, the next week we were down at the *Old Cock and Bull* for a knees-up – Scotty Jock's leaving-do, I think it was. He'd been with us since before the year dot, you know. Keeper of the Keys and Master of the Evidence Lock-Up – at least, that was his job for as long as I knew him. Mention he'd been on the beat once upon a time, but that was so long ago it must've been with Sir Robert's very own plod-squad!"

"So what happened? What was special about this particular send-off?"

"Not the send-off, not as such. It wasn't that. What I recall is the grand old sing-song we had: *Knees Up Mother Brown, Maybe It's Because I'm A Londoner, It's a Long Way To Tipperary* – you know, the standard fare and the usual fodder?"

"Indeed I do!"

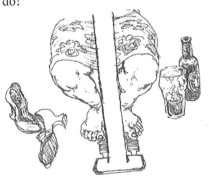

"But it wasn't the songs themselves, nor the well-oiled voices of the choir, as mellifluous as any gathered in the Valleys boy-o, no – it was the band, see. It was those fellows, one on bass and the other on Grand Piano like, it was the combo, Bazz and Rave, on bass and keyboards respectively. Now of course we were expecting no less but we did not imagine anything more than an old honky-tonk piano at best. When we saw this beautiful G.P. and heard Bazz tinkling the ivories and ebonies, we were inspired!"

I imagined the scene: DeVille and Saunders, off-duty, hair down; Chief Inspector, an early appearance and a judicious early departure immediately after the eulogy and presentation; Scotty Jock – the man himself – embarrassed, tongue-tied, wishing he were somewhere else – and then the band setting off on a rambling verse and chorus that somehow miraculously re-formed itself into something very much like *"I've been a Wild Rover...*

I could not imagine how She felt. The Steinway, with such high hopes and ambitions, with such reasonable expectations of preferment, brought tumbling down to earth with a crash! Here She was, forced to entertain the drunken crowd with common tunes and crude melodies. It was not until well after midnight that the choir began to disperse and wend its way homeward. It was not until after more than an hour later that silence and darkness finally settled on the stage.

When She woke, in the chill of an autumn morning, She found herself loosed from her moorings once again and mysteriously deposited dockside by the Thames.

BBC Breakfast News:

"And now we go over to our Classical Music Reporter, Jaladyce Burns-Wood:"

"Thank you James. Yes, we are here in the wastelands of the old Royal Albert Docks. All around the new-builds of converted warehouses stare down upon us, but here, here we see the last vestiges of the Blitz. The Royal Albert Docks are the last surviving symbol of a once thriving trade in Scandinavian timber. And it was here, today, that an

unexpected castaway was recovered. This stolen Harrods Steinway was found, by a small boy on his bicycle, precisely here at Number Nine Dockside." (Pan right, zoom in on piano and boy)."

Pictures showed her curvaceous legs were scratched and her white keys were a dusty red colour – It looked as if she'd been dragged through a bush backwards – which she had. When the reporter played the ragged keys, it was clear she was in dire need of re-tuning.

Displayed on national television for all to see, this was certainly one mortified *Joanna*! Although she was subsequently re-polished and returned to Harrods, she did not take up her previous pride of place. Instead, she was sold off at half price in the January Sales.

Harrods has since reviewed its operational procedures and the Stores Department are no longer permitted to weigh anchor and remove items without the appropriate paperwork. Of course, this does not mean that items will not be removed but, if they are, it will have been done contrary to established procedures.

I asked DeVille what he made of this outcome. He replied, somewhat enigmatically, that whoever paid the piper called the tune. I felt in my pocket and found just enough cash to pay for another round. When I returned with the drinks DeVille was, unusually, paused in his restless narrative. For a moment there was stillness, an uncertain quiet; there was jeopardy.

And then he continued ...

The Good Samaritans

The Good Samaritan carries out his humanitarian task without giving any thought to the consequences. Whether it is a reflex action or an act born of long and quiet contemplation, we may not know. But whatever the case, the Good Samaritan acts regardless of the consequences. He is altruistic, humanly-bound, and acting on an ethical instinct when he steps in to assist, to provide succour, to help his fellow human being. We may consider him foolish but we cannot doubt his sincerity or his endeavour. In the case of those professionally directed to provide assistance, the case is perhaps less clear. Some might say it is merely a matter of duty. I am inclined to disagree.

Our story begins in a Grade 2 listed building or, more precisely, a suite of cubicles, a public urinal, a desperate destination for all the unwary whose bladders ambush them. This listed building is to be found in the vicinity of Old Holborn and is much frequented by occasional visitors and regulars alike. In this Grade 2 listed building there are some rather interesting and distinctive architectural elements. In particular, and quite apart from any *Art Deco* design features, the high-level water closets are made of a transparent glass. It is possible to see the full workings of the flush-and-refill mechanism. However, that is not all that may be seen, for someone has introduced fishes into these tanks. They are home to a number of varieties of goldfish from Shubunkin to Lionhead, from Fantail to Black Moor.

Today there is a man who has collapsed in a cubicle in the vicinity of Old Holborn. A call comes out to the Panda car. Unit Seven, a pair of London's finest on foot, walkabout, runabout, anywhere-on-demand, Panda-equipped, uniformed coppers, rushes to the rescue. The poor unfortunate fellow appears to be somewhat worse for wear but does not seem to have had a heart-attack or banged his head. Nonetheless Unit Seven help him into the Panda car and take him swiftly to the A&E Department at University College Hospital (UCH) where they dutifully deposit him into the care of other professionals.

Good deed and duty done they make their way back to the station and retire to the staff canteen. Deville notices his partner scratching his rear end indiscreetly. His own left leg responds with a sympathetic itching. Much as yawning is a spontaneous social reflex, so too is itching and the scratching of that itch. I do not know how long their standard tea break was but I presume no more than ten or fifteen minutes. What I do know however, is that before the break was over, PC DeVille and his partner were summoned to the Sergeant's desk and told to report immediately to A&E up at Euston, no questions asked, pronto, without delay and as quick as you can: "*And that's an order!*"

DeVille continues his story:

"So off we drive in the Panda car to A&E. We were there within the hour, easily. Anyway, when we arrive we are greeted by a senior nurse of the no-nonsense variety.

"Ah gentlemen! So glad you could come. How are you? Feeling alright? I expect you want to know how our patient is doing, after all you were so kind as to bring him in to us. Well, when I came to move him from the drying room to a bed on the ward – let me tell you – the floor suddenly heaved and twitched rapidly, like the crack of a shammy leather. I have never seen so many lice in all my born days! Enough to make anyone itch to death, I wouldn't wonder. But we've fumigated everything – several times – and dealt withal the patient's infected clothing. In fact we've dealt

with all clothing except *your* uniforms. If you could just step this way we'll soon have that sorted."

"We followed, somewhat sheepishly, into a small room where we stripped off right down to our birthday suits and were duly fumigated most thoroughly. I thought of Winscale and nuclear accidents and fierce scrubbing-downs in the decontamination unit. This was far worse," DeVille explained, "Our uniforms, shirts, vests, pants and socks were put into the incinerator straightaway, without any undue ceremony and never mind fumigation! Only our shiny boots were spared. Then we were sent home in make-do boiler suits."

Now in those days we were both living at the Police Hostel and we only had two uniforms each, so to lose one was pretty serious. We called the Sergeant and explained our predicament. He was none too pleased with us, especially as the Panda car had had to be thoroughly fumigated with three separate Vesuvius bombs! He told us not to come back for the rest of the shift. In fact he said:

"I don't want to see you two lousy pair of sheep again till you're dipped, shorn and shining!"

Needless to say, we did as we were told and did not report for duty till the next day.

Now you may wonder, as I did, what the moral of this story is. Is it that the Good Samaritan will have his reward in Heaven but be treated like poor Job whilst here on Earth? Or is it that following duty is no guarantee of honourable recognition but, on the contrary, may confer pariah status? I prefer to consider the story as depicting an ironic view of the world.

By the way, is it just me, or are you itching too?

Confession of a Master Car Thief

Deville called last night. Had I heard the story of the car thief, the one locked up at Her Majesty's Pleasure, who had been "holidaying" on the Isle of Wight? I hadn't? Did I have a moment now? I did.

"I was based in Kensington at the time. I took a call from a fellow officer in the Hampshire Constabulary. A Detective Sergeant Williams whose role was that of prison liaison officer. He was making enquiries. Did I have an up-to-date list of thefts from cars parked in our London area over the last five to ten years? Yes, we did have one, but I'd have to speak to the Desk Sergeant who would know where it was *hidden*."

"So what do you need that for?" I asked.

And D.S. Williams began to explain:

"Well, it's like this – though you won't believe it, I'm sure."

"Try me," said Deville.

"Alright then. We've got this fellow in prison here who wants to tell us about his record, I mean his *full* record, of thefts from cars."

"What's his name?" Deville enquired.

"Teddy Trinder. Heard of him?"

"Can't say as I have. I might know his brother though. Go on."

"Well, he is writing up the details. We already have fully itemised accounts of nearly a hundred thefts and that's only for the last couple of years. He's got information for us going back maybe ten years."

DeVile's interest was piqued. If this were true, then the Golden Goose would soon be coming home to lay. The monthly solved crime statistics (SCS) would be off the scale!

"Okay, here's what we'll do. You fax me through some details for a few different times and places and I'll get the records for comparison. If the information looks good then we can take it further."

So that is what they agreed to do. The information did indeed prove good. Every one of the cases that Williams passed over to DeVille tallied with the crime reports – these were the hand-written records of all unsolved cases. DeVille explained:

"The crime reports were known as either *Black Inkers* or *Red Inkers*. The *Black Inkers* were for unsolved crimes and recorded information about the crime and any investigations undertaken subsequently. The *Red Inkers* were the solved crimes where the name of the accused was recorded, in red ink. Of course, if the Court found the accused not guilty then it became a *Black Inker* again."

"Sounds a bit like the wheelbarrow I met as I was going up!" I said.

"Precisely!" said DeVille. Anyway, I spoke to the Super', who was equally enthusiastic about the chance of boosting the SCS figures. He had one suggestion. That they should distribute their findings across several months' figures so they didn't have one bumper period that made all subsequent ones look feeble by comparison.

That's probably why he made Detective Superintendent and I didn't. Well, that and the golf, I suppose."

"Golf?" I asked, a bit slow on the uptake.

"Yes, schmoozing with the big-wigs on Home Counties golf courses. Part of the job really. Don't get me wrong, the Super', as he was affectionately known by all, was a good bloke. One of the best. Always backed his officers. But it was a part of the job I could never be any good at. I speak my mind too readily. That reminds me. To his face we always addressed him as Detective Superintendent or Sir. One of my young trainee detectives – I think it was Robinson – once made the mistake of calling him Super'. For a moment the world stopped."

"It's *Detective Superintendent* to you, laddie!"

"Yes, Sir. Sorry Sir – Detective Superintendent."

"So anyway, the Super' authorised a travel warrant and I went down to Southampton by train from Waterloo, and then took the Red Funnel ferry across to Cowes on the island."

"Did you take the tube train on the pier when you arrived?" I asked.

"No, that's at Ryde. That's the Portsmouth to Ryde ferry."

"Of course."

"Yes, I remember going there as a kid on a Sunday School

outing," said DeVille. Funny to find a tube train there but it was running like a shuttle-train, I suppose. We spent most of the day playing on the beach and swimming in the sea."

DeVille indulged himself in a moment's nostalgic memory. I imagined he was transported back there, busy building sandcastles that he decorated with brightly coloured paper flags stuck atop matchwood poles.

"Where was I? Oh yes, I remember. You know there are three prisons on the Island, designed for different category prisoners. I suppose the most famous one is Parkhurst – that's where they keep the really serious criminals, the violent and dangerous ones particularly. Of course, the Isle of Wight is a bit like Alcatraz you know."

I didn't know. "How so? I asked, "Is it full of film stars?"

"Very droll. No, it's surrounded by treacherous tides and man-eating sharks, don't you know?"

"I see," I said, smiling ruefully.

"But there are two other prisons," explained DeVille, "One of them was an open prison, designed for low risk prisoners nearing the end of their sentence. That's where I met Teddy Trinder. My first impressions were of a rather small and insignificant man, middle-aged (about forty-five), with a receding hairline and bright blue eyes beneath bushy eyebrows. He may have had an aquiline nose for all it mattered but nothing struck me as special about his nose. Of course, I knew better than to judge merely by appearances."

"So what did he have to say for himself?" I asked.

"What didn't he have to say, more like. Sang like a bloomin' canary. You would have heard him from pit-head, all the way down the main shaft, and as far as the furthest seam. If I'd been a coal-miner he'd have come with me on every shift."

"So was he a miner then?" I enquired.

"Well, not exactly, though he did come from Durham way originally. I found that out later, when I knew him much better. At first he just wanted to tell me about his numerous exploits as a professional car thief – that's what he called it – *professional*.

"I see," I said, "*Professional*, eh?"

"Yes, and he certainly was. But there were a couple of questions I needed answers to first:

Q.1. Why was he confessing now?

Q.2. How did he remember all his crimes in such perfect detail?

It was the prison guard who provided an answer to the first question. Apparently Teddy had sent his girlfriend several *Visitor Slips* but she hadn't come to see him. Worse than that, he had found out from a former cell-mate, who was now back on the outside, that she was selling off his pension fund. Do you know what that was?"

I shook my head, even though we were not on a video call and DeVille couldn't see my response. But he took my silence as a 'no' anyway and continued apace:

"It was all the jewellery he'd stolen – small valuable, items like gold cufflinks and diamond rings, that sort of stuff. He'd been hanging on to some of it as an investment for his eventual retirement. I mean he could hardly go and purchase an annuity now, could he? What's more, all these valuables were hidden in the frame of his brass bed. Simply unscrew the top from the tubing – oh and turn the bed upside-down and give it a shake. It would all just come tumbling out, every item neatly labelled with a time, place, and date. Most meticulous, our Teddy was."

"So he'd fallen out with his girlfriend, I see that, but what was he hoping for by giving her up and the remains of his pension fund too?" I asked, rather puzzled.

"Well now, that's the clever bit. Or not so clever, depending how you look at it. He was hell-bent on revenge. He was losing his earnings – well, their joint earnings, as it happened – I'll explain later – and he wasn't going to have that, was he? He'd selected his *nuclear option*. He was going to take her down with him and hope for leniency for himself in any sentence delivered by the court. After all, he was very co-operative – that was undeniable, if a bit late in the day!

As I sat and quizzed Teddy it became obvious that he had a photographic and encyclopaedic memory. I had persuaded the Super' to let me bring some of the crime reports with me so that cross-checking could be done in situ. This was definitely a time-saver though I still had a fair bit of homework to do later updating the records fully in the obligatory red ink required for the job. That first day we covered over a hundred cases, all confirmed. And we did the same again the next day. Eventually we had more than four hundred cases cross-checked and *red-inked*, marked down as solved."

"What about all the other stolen goods, the stuff he hadn't hidden away for his pension?" I asked, "Did you ask him how he'd got rid of that?"

"Yes, I did. Most of it he had fenced, of course, but he wouldn't tell me who his 'slaughters' were?"

"His 'slaughters'? What are they?" I asked.

"The people he'd sold stuff to, stuff that he'd nicked. His *fences*, if you like. They were known as slaughters in the trade. Criminal slang."

"I see." I made a mental note to google the term later.

"The funny thing was that he did tell me a couple of names", said DeVille.

"Why was that?" I asked.

"Well, he explained that there were a couple of guys who'd ripped him off. Seems a bit rich, I know, but honour among thieves an' all that. Anyway, he took great delight in paying them back and we did eventually recover some of the stuff he'd nicked and sold on."

"All part of his nuclear option, I suppose?"

"That's right. If he was going down he'd take others with him, no qualms or quibbles. Anyway, that same evening I phoned the Super' to update him on our progress. I told him I was on my way back up to town with Sergeant Williams. The next morning we wasted no time in going to Teddy's place armed with a search warrant. Sure enough we found the stolen items in the tubing of the metal-framed bed. And not only there but also in his stepson's bedframe. He was a piece of work that lad and that's no lie. A real mouth on him. I warned him but he wouldn't back off. So in the end we arrested him too, as an accomplice after the fact. Later there was the court case, of course. Teddy got eighteen months to run concurrently but his girlfriend got the full five years. That wasn't all."

There's more?" I asked in disbelief.

"There certainly is more. I got to know Teddy a lot better over time. In fact I came rather to respect his professionalism. I mean, he took pride in his work and was b...y good at it. After his early release on parole he approached me for a bit of help with the Social Security forms and he needed some sort of character reference for a job. Anyway, always willing to help someone back onto the straight and narrow, I decided to kill two birds with one stone."

"I've never actual seen that done but I did once see a country lad kill a bird in the hedge with a large pebble. He just threw it like a speeding missile," I remarked.

"Have you now?" said DeVille with mock curiosity.

"Anyway, I had a bit of a brainwave. I had been asked to do some lecturing at Trainee Detective Night School. I thought I'd invite Teddy to come along as a guest speaker. He was an instant success. After his first appearance I had a chat with the lads and explained his situation. They all agreed to an extra-mural class where they'd each chip in a couple of quid to help pay his expenses. I called in a favour and we booked a room in Red Lion Square, free of charge, every week on a Wednesday for a whole month. I don't think I ever learnt so much about the true art of car theft, in particular the secret keeping of stolen jewellery in a pair of clean y-fronts. The trainee detectives couldn't believe their eyes and their ears. Teddy didn't look at all like a car thief (What did one look like?) and he didn't behave like one either (lingering, looking about, shifty). His *modus operandi* was generally as follows: His girlfriend would "mark" cars as she walked along the other side of the street. Perhaps she stopped to adjust her headscarf or maybe she looked at her watch. And they would always go for cars that had parked up to go to a restaurant or to the cinema or near the West End shops. They knew the driver would not be returning for a while. They never stole from more than two or three vehicles in one area and they shifted their territory every week. Teddy always made sure his own car was fully insured, taxed, and MOT'd. He carried the papers in the car with him. This was to avoid problems if he were ever stopped by the police. But his master stroke was – well, a "stroke"! He wore a blue wrist band that showed he had an unspecified but serious illness. On the few occasions Teddy did get stopped by Policeman Plod he would feign fainting, as it were, or fake a fit. An ambulance would be called immediately, no questions asked. Once in hospital Teddy would quietly discharge himself, forgetting to tell the staff at the admin desk. But I can't tell you all the real tricks of the trade or I'll be giving you ideas!"

"And not just me," I said, "Your readers too!"

"Quite so! Anyway, I'd better finish up now. Just to say that this was the biggest win we'd ever had by way of clearing up cold-cases. The Super was positively dancing with joy when I arrived back at the office late in the afternoon. He even broke open a bottle of the finest malt whisky and poured me a generous glass. Mind you, he was none too pleased later that evening when he returned to his car after a Charity Gala dinner at the Guildhall. He found that someone had broken into his vehicle and stolen a case of his best Scottish Malt from the trunk. But that was on a Wednesday evening and Teddy had more than a dozen trainee detectives providing an alibi."

Archie and the Cricket

Archie – mad as a hatter but dedicated to the cause – that's what it was for him. You'd never think he was in the Force. He was too cool, too eccentric, too likeable, to be one of the Met's best detectives. He was undercover more often than not. Long hair was *de rigeur* in those days. He had an English father and a French mother. As a result he naturally grew up bi-lingual. He once spent three months on duty in a French prison cell, alongside a UK drug dealer. He never suspected that Archie wasn't anything but French. Archie was worried he might talk in his sleep and give himself away. But he never did. It was the drug dealer who dished up the dirt on the rest of the gang, *el Capo* included.

After leaving the Police Force, Archie retired to the South of France, where he toured the local restaurants and bars with his harmonica and guitar, singing a mixture of traditional English & French folk songs. He was, I suppose, one of the last of the old troubadours.

Recently he had returned to the U.K. to settle some family business and was staying at his cousin's near Richmond. He had been due to go fishing with DeVille and his brother but had cried off, saying he felt unwell. That was on the Friday. Saturday morning he died suddenly of a heart attack. Nearly a thousand people attended his funeral. Three of his former girlfriends were there; he had no ex-wives. All three sat together on a windswept rainy afternoon somewhere on the edge of Wimbledon Common. All were in tears. They consoled each other in their mutual grief.

DeVille wanted me to hear the eulogy delivered at Archie's funeral, on the day they did their very best to give him a fitting send off. It would be necessary to pull out all the stops – diapason, drone, coupler etc., dismiss all common convention, and swear blind irreverence to formality, orthodoxy and respectability. It must be an occasion of complete celebration, of recognition of the man and his unique contribution to the work of the Met. But beyond that, the way he had enriched everybody's life. It must be a fitting tribute to the genius of an eccentric and incorruptible detective. To this end the eulogy was designed to show Archie in full swing, at his most outlandish, at his funniest, at his very best.

"I remember, we were at a conference at the Police College in Henley. Archie was delivering a talk on the nature of undercover work, in which he was an acknowledged expert. He was generous with his experience and was always seeking to further the understanding of others. But he didn't suffer fools gladly. And that day was a prime example.

One of the Senior Officers attending Archie's lecture, a Deputy Chief Constable, as it happened, asked a question which, if had been listening more carefully, he need not have asked. However, Archie responded generously and explained the point once again. But these interruptions continued, from the same source. On the third occasion Archie stopped himself as he was about to answer. Instead he reaches inside his jacket and carefully pulls out a box of *Bryant & May* safety matches. This he places on top of the lectern in front of him. Then he taps lightly on the matchbox. Slowly the box opens and a small golden-coloured cricket seems to hop onto Archie's hand."

"*Ladies and gentlemen, let me introduce my friend Clive.*

Clive is a Cricket. We first met when I found him trapped in a piece of prehistoric amber in an old curio shop in Melsham."

Archie holds Clive close to his ear.

"Sorry, what's that you say Clive? That man wasn't listening properly? No he wasn't, was he."

Archie continued his talk, placing Clive on top of his match box on top of the lectern. After a few moments there was another interruption. Once again Archie picked up Clive, the fossilised Cricket, and spoke to him:

"Yes Clive? That same man still isn't listening? No, he isn't, is he. You think anyone who had been listening would know the answer to that question? Do you know the answer? Yes, you do. Ok will you tell us the answer? No? Why not? I see, because we should have been listening. Right."

After a short while the Deputy Chief Constable raises his hand once again and says:

"Do you know who I am?"

Without a moment's hesitation Archie picks up Clive and places him in the palm of his hand once again:

"Clive, do you know who he is? I see you're shaking your head. So you don't know who he is then. Well neither does he, it seems. Yes, yes, that is a bit worrying, isn't it. What's that?

You think we should get him some help? He might have had a nasty bump on the head?"

At that moment the Deputy Chief Constable got up and stormed out of the lecture theatre, accompanied by an uncontrollable eruption of uncontainable laughter.

"Alright everyone, Clive wants to hear the rest of what I've go to say."

And with a straight face, none straighter, Archie continued to deliver his unforgettable lecture on undercover operations while Clive the Cricket sat and listened attentively, along with everyone else in the theatre.

Later, at the bar, we drank a toast to Archie and thanked Clive for putting the Deputy Chief Constable in his rightful place. Clive was somewhat abashed to receive such praise for his efforts. He bowed humbly:

"What's that you say, Clive? It was nothing? Of course. Another round? Absolutely! The drinks are on me," said Archie.

Gorilla Tactics

"It's a jungle out there," DeVille began, "and I don't just mean that metaphorically."

"How so?" I enquired, without any consideration for my own safety.

"Well it's the concrete – the high-rise blocks and the backstreet shacks and the corrugated shanties. And then there's the lock-ups and alleyways, the old red brick and the broken mains just off the dilapidated High St. It's everyman for himself out there and woe betide the innocent man – though are few enough around here – woe betide the innocent man, I say, who falls prey to their devious ways and their wicked guiles. Even the traveling tinkers aren't safe around here!"

And so DeVille began to describe the world that, in those not so distant days, was the London village of Melsham. It was his world too, one into which he ventured on each relief, each tour of duty, day or night. It was his own personal Vietnam in which he did battle with both the local peoples and the rigid orthodoxy of the Chief Constable and his (very) Senior Officers. It was a constant struggle and one which might sap your strength if you weren't careful to maintain an inner distance from the small matters of duty, process and protocol.

But he was not alone. Engaged alongside DeVille in the battle against wickedness and folly, was Davey, *Daft Davey*, as he was affectionately known. And daft he certainly was but true as a nail, hard as granite, and more trustworthy than a heart surgeon.

"I'd trust Davey with my life any day – in fact I have," claimed DeVille, and I for one was certainly ready to believe him.

But he left us wondering and did not, at that time, elaborate further. Later we learnt that Davey was daft by design. It gave him an advantage, or that's what DeVille told us. Davey was deceiving, though not deceitful; he was charming though not phony; he was sometimes a bit zany and occasionally bordered on downright crazy but he was a really decent bloke for all that, one of the best.

I have written elsewhere of DeVille's philosophical musing on, and practical application of, the skill of interviewing (*On Interviewing As One Of The Fine Arts*). I shall not repeat here all that I have previously described. Instead I will try to show the combined effectiveness of DeVille's composure and Davey's counterpoint improvisation. I will give you an example – let me just to refer to my notes ...

Imagine the scene, if you will. We are in Interview Room Seven (IR7). DeVille is interviewing. He is interviewing an old lag, a familiar face, a career criminal. DeVille is accompanied only by a constable standing on security at the door. The interview is, of course, being recorded – for training purposes etc. and begins at 10:47 a.m. DeVille knows that his interviewee knows that he knows that the old lag is a professional who knows the game. But he doesn't know that DeVille knows all about the interview process and its infinite subtlety and variety. However, what DeVille doesn't know is that *Davey* is about to subvert the whole carefully designed charade.

DeVille continues:

"So you were not at 55, Acacia Avenue on the occasion of the burglary last Sunday evening. You were in fact attending a service of praise at the Sutton and Cheam Pentecostal church?"

"Correct."

"And you have never been to The Old Vicarage by the common?" continued DeVille.

"No, never. I've never been Church of England me!"

"But you are, clearly, a god-fearing man?"

"Oh yes. I'm a sinner alright, in need of redemption. I know that much."

DeVille was beginning to feel that his skills and experience must be starting to dull. He needed to sharpen up his approach and shift up a gear or two. However, that proved unnecessary, as it happened. How did it happen? Well, at that moment there was a knock on the door and a gorilla entered the room. Well, DeVille knew it was Davey, of course, but the old lag saw only a gorilla who, saying absolutely nothing, proceeded to sit down and examine a banana. DeVille continued, totally unperturbed. Without missing a beat he asked why his counterpart sat agog and speechless.

"B...b...but that's a gorilla there!"

"Excuse me? Where? I can't see one. It's just you me and the constable here. Now please answer the question. Did you or did you not commit this burglary?" DeVille continued, completely straight-faced.

The gorilla proceeded, slowly, to peel the banana. He took a bite. Then he offered it to the suspect opposite. He declined. The gorilla continued to devour the delicious banana. DeVille continued to keep a straight face – just about – goodness knows how!

Now of course this was a serious problem for the old lag being interviewed under suspicion of burglary. I mean, no-one would believe him if he said he'd been interviewed by Inspector DeVille and a gorilla. They'd think he was mad! Whatever might happen he did not want to be sent to the funny farm. And of course DeVille understood his dilemma, his quandary, his somewhat difficult position. He said nothing and merely paused for a while. Then Davey got up to leave and the PC at the door saluted as he left.

The game was up. Yes, 55 Acacia Avenue. That was right. The Pentecostal church was the Sunday before. By the time the duty solicitor arrived it was all done and dusted with a signed confession and three other charges to be taken into consideration.

Of course you will not find this particular interview technique described in any of the official manuals. And indeed it never actually happened. Who would believe it? Later that afternoon DeVille saw Davey in the queue at the canteen.

"Hey, nice one Davey!, he said.

Davey turned and smiled, "Why's that?" He asked innocently.

"You know, the gorilla stunt. That was genius!"

"Sorry DeVille, not sure what you're talking about. You been overdoing it?"

"Come on, the gorilla tactic that you used in my interview this afternoon. Marvellous!"

"Not sure what you mean, old chap. I've been giving evidence up at the Old Bailey all day. Been there since half past nine. Just got back about half an hour ago."

DeVille was first surprised and then disbelieving. Davey placed a cup and saucer on his tray, pressed a button for *white tea, two sugars*, took a banana from the fruit basket on the counter, and then he moved on to the checkout. DeVille followed, with a pot of tea and a packet of two stem-ginger biscuits. As they sat opposite each other someone else came and sat at the table next to them. It was a gorilla. DeVille glanced at Davey. He decided he would be well advised to take a sip of malt from the bottle that he kept, for medicinal purposes, such as this, at the back of the top drawer of his desk, under a well-thumbed copy of *Crime and Punishment*. He offered Davey a glass as well. Perhaps the gorilla would care to join them for a wee dram?

The London Village of Melsham (Part 1)

There are certain parts of London that have never really left behind their original village identities. This is especially true as we venture further away from the City and into Greater London. My grandfather grew up in Beckenham, for example and I recall that my great-grandmother always used to say that she lived in Beckenham Village.

However, there is another characteristic of settled rural communities that, remarkably, is still evident in parts of London. Although we may think of the great metropolis as a mixing-pot of many different peoples and nations, of giving rise to diversity and variety, it also contains certain pockets of repetition and insularity. One such place is the former village of Melsham, situated on the outskirts of the centre of London. Melsham is not untypical. It has: a common, a train station, a village green, and a High Street. There is a choice of chapels and, recently, a Roman Catholic Church, located in a converted folly in the grounds of one of its two great houses. It is here that we may discover a curious stock of humanity. It is neither homogenous nor unique, neither intelligent nor stupid. It is merely incredible. Whether this is the result of particular repeating sequences in certain chains of DNA no-one knows but it is strongly suspected by some, including Dr McKindlay, who has served the local population to the best of his ability for the last fifty years at least.

One evening I received a call from DeVille. I can't remember if he was responding to an earlier call from me or whether I had called him but the important thing is what he told me: more stories about the London village of Melsham.

'When I met Dr McKindlay he was nearing the end of his career. He must have been all of eighty then, though he only admitted to being in his late sixties. He was a very tall man but without a stoop, and was completely bald. He knew Melsham inside out and the people in the area likewise. His tales of local doings and dealings would beggar belief; I always took what he said with a pinch of salt and a tincture of sloe tonic. But it was what I witnessed with my own two eyes that made me realise the Doc's stories were not as farfetched as they seemed.

I was out on patrol with my mate Jimmy, constable White, one very warm summer evening. I hadn't known Jimmy long but we got on well. We had the same sense of humour, sort of droll but cheerful. Anyway, we were in the Panda car. A call came in about some trouble at the local chippy. As we headed off to investigate I spied a suspicious vehicle. Now you may say, correctly, that I was suspicious *of* the vehicle. That would be true. But what I mean is that it looked *iffy* to me. I had seen a couple of lads and a dog in the car. On this occasion one of the lads was driving. I said to Jimmy:

"Let's just take a look at this lot, shall we?"

As we pulled alongside, the lads gave us two-fingered salutes. At first the dog seemed more respectful until it suddenly stuck its tongue out at us. Then the driver gave it some wellie and the chase was on.

"Right, we'll have this lot." I said, "Follow that car!"

I always like saying that, you know?

"Right-e-o Sarge!" said Jimmy.

Off we sped in hot pursuit, blue light flashing and siren sounding. The full works. When we got to the common they turned down a dirt track before coming to a locked metal five-bar gate. Almost before they had screeched to a halt the two lads bolted, hurdling the gate head-first, leaving the dog behind.

We chased them as far as we could – well as far as the gate anyway. Then we turned and went back to the car. The numpties had left their passenger behind and it wasn't wearing a seat-belt.

"Alright mate, your nicked," I said to the dog.

"The dog looked at me soulfully with strange-eyes, it had a white coat and sported a white pointy beard."

"Sarge?" said Jimmy.

"Yes," I replied.

"I don't think it's a dog."

"What do you mean?" I said, "Have I arrested the wrong one?"

"No Sarge!" Jimmy said, "Take another look."

I then looked more closely. Jimmy was right. It wasn't a dog. For one thing its tail was too short and for another it had horns, and a beard, and its dark pupils stared back at us with a haunting horizontal gaze. What's more, it had chewed through the back of the driver's seat and was proceeding to eat the road atlas, floormats, and First Aid kit as well. It was in fact a goat, undoubtedly. Yes, that's right, a goat. By the time our police goat-handler – I mean *dog*-handler – arrived to take the goat to the pound, we were a bit late getting to the chippy. But let me tell you what happened when we did eventually get there."

No problem at his premises, the owner told us, but there had been an incident, about half an hour ago, round the corner at the neighbouring chicken burger bar. So we went round the corner to the aforementioned chicken burger bar.

"And what did you find there?" I asked.

'I'll tell you what we found there. We found a smashed shopfront and a number plate, and a couple of young chaps both a bit shaken up. They were counter staff and were starting to clear up the debris. They were our witnesses, of course.'

"So what had happened?"

'Funny you should ask me that 'cause that's exactly what I wanted to know at the time. But let me wind back a bit first.'

"Alright, please do," I said.

"*Wilco*," replied DeVille and continued from the point to which he had rewound the story.

'Let me tell you about Hiram Harris. Or rather, why don't we let Doc McKindlay tell us about Hiram the highwayman, a gypsy of fixed abode, terror of Melsham Common and the doyen of all the fair damsels of that parish. This is what the good doctor told me:'

"Harris? Hiram Harris? What do you want to know?" asked Dr McKinlay.

"Well, we know he ram-raided the chicken burger bar because he left his number-plate behind. The DVLA records confirmed that much," Deville explained.

"I see," said Dr McKindlay.

"Of course he was never actually one of my patients, you understand. No, he was a regular at A&E but coughs and colds were never his ailments. What I can tell you about Mr H. Harris is based solely on what I have seen and heard over the years. Some of it may be falsehood, some may be exaggeration, and some may even be true. You must judge for yourself."

"Of course," said DeVille, professionally

"You see Hiram Harris was one of those men who pleases themselves first and last – and may the devil take the hindmost! Good in a fight, better as a friend, and mostly a maker of as many enemies as you can shake a shillelagh at! You must understand that he was very much of these parts, generation unto generation, as you might say. He was a very local person with a very local mixture of genes and means. By all accounts he was none too bright but reliably belligerent. I'll give you an example."

'Well, the good doctor gave an unequivocal descriptive illustration of the ancient martial and Romany art of *Shindig*. This involved fists and curses and shenanigans, as well the aforementioned shillelaghs. He continued in this vein for some while, providing us with as good a character reference as you may wish for when submitting a case for the *prosecution*.'

"But it's getting late now, I should let you go," said DeVille.

But he didn't, of course. He continued – though briefly, as we did indeed all need to go. His summary was that Hiram Harris, land-locked gypsy, parish-bound wanderer with footwear made in equal measure of leather and lead, whose perspectives and horizons were as imaginative as the handcrafted hobnails in his well-worn boots, did not amuse the local magistrate. Far from it. Three months imprisonment and, over on the common by the pond, a day in the stocks!

The London Village of Melsham (Part 2)

Earlier today I received a text message from DeVille. He had some material for the next episode, having consulted Dr McKindlay once again. Although the good Doc was by now at least a hundred years old, his memory was as sharp as a cut-throat razor and could be relied upon far more than DeVille's or my own, and I have not yet reached retirement age.

But before I go on, I should say something more about the place and the people of this particular, not to say peculiar, London village. I first met Dr McKindlay only recently and this is how he described Melsham to me:

"I suppose the Common is the most well-known feature, but you mustn't forget the Greens."

"Greens?" I asked.

"Yes, Greens. Not cabbage or kale – no, the Greens."

I waited for him while he thought. He continued to think. I waited. I began to wonder if he might have unexpectedly expired but then, at last, he spoke again:

"Aye, there were the two Greens, you see? There was the Fair Green and there was the Dark Green, where they played cricket. I was once asked to umpire on the Dark Green you know. But I'm more of a *shinty* man myself. Born and bred in the Highlands, that's me. Still I managed to carry it off and my performance on the day seemed to be acceptable. Of course it was the local team that won the match. As for the Fair Green, well that was a once-a-year affair, by ancient Royal Charter, dating back beyond *Domesday*. That was a more boisterous affair and there was no way that annual event could be umpired. It always resulted in my becoming very busy some nine months later."

I was on the point of asking in more detail about home deliveries but the Doctor continued apace:

"Did I mention the Races? No, I thought not. This was a matter of gigging across the East/West diagonal of the Common.

The local gypsy folk loved their horses, of course. And they loved their racing. But most of all they loved their betting. Now, the races between the Red House and the Blue House were the most sporting of all these races across the hypotenuse. Though the Red House was not red and the Blue house was not blue. It was a straight course, undulating with hidden dips, but the rules of fair racing were never more evident than in their absence. It was a veritable chariot race worthy of the Romans themselves. And their dogs too. Great bristling hounds that bounded alongside. Aye, a sight to behold, that's for sure!

One of the keenest giggers was Hiram Harris himself, the self-styled *Melsham Highwayman* – though I never knew of a robbery on Melsham Common in all my years. But he was most famous as an all-round bruiser and a man with an insatiable appetite for bareknuckle fights and barroom brawls.

Hiram was banned from the *Iron Crown* and the *Merry Monk* alike though he thought nothing of marching in to either pub and demanding the means of quenching his lusty thirst. But it was at the *Spoon & Star* that he made his grandest entrance one night and proceeded to hurl a stool through the plate glass at the back of the bar. Needless to say, the landlord was quick to call the Old Bill and, it being their local, they were equally quick to respond.

Now it just so happened that Old Tombstone was seated in the snug at the back of the bar by the fire when they arrived – the coppers in uniform, that is. Abraham Tombstone, patriarch of the place, father of generations of Melsham spawn, one-toothed wonder of the snag-toothed populace of the village of old Melsham. There he sat and spied it all: the smashed glass, the landlord sweeping, the landlady weeping, the plain-clothes officers of the CID gathering at the bar to order their drinks, and the reappearing figure of his great-nephew Hiram Harris, returned from his hiding place in the old people's care home over the road, thinking the police had departed. Well of course Uniform had indeed dispersed to search for him far and wide. However, Hiram had not reckoned on the raincoated gentlemen now occupying seats at the bar, who were the non-uniformed and well-placed colleagues of the boys in blue."

DeVille takes up the story:

"That's right Doc. I remember he came storming back in cussing and swearing and shouting "I'm gonna wreck this place!"

Only then he sees us fellows at the bar, six non-uniformed "gavvers", as he would say."

"Gavvers?" I asked.

"That's right, cause we're the ones who *gavver 'em up*, all the miscreants and ne'er-do-wells, the troublemakers – it's a gypsy term of endearment, you know.

Hiram was a big lad and quite a handful, I tell you. But once Jimmy sat on him he couldn't move. The funny thing was, when Uniform returned, empty handed, they were a bit nonplussed as to how we'd managed to find him, subdue him, and arrest him while they were out and about searching high and low to no avail. Then I heard Old Tombstone laughing and cackling over by the fireplace. He was dancing a crooked jig of delight and seemed to find the whole episode quite hilarious.

Now talking of horses, pony and trap and the like, I must tell you about a particular horse. I don't know how many hands, though he had four feet, but he wasn't a Shetland or some tiny variety like that. Well, this horse was nothing special to look at as such. It's just where it was. Sometimes we found ourselves out in the fields searching for body parts; inquisitive horses would sometimes come and shake their heads at us or, occasionally, nod as if in approval. More often than not though we were in an urban environment and our detective work involved plenty of house to house calls or, in this case, flat to flat. The lift was out of order at Watchers Tower and I'm not sure it had ever been in order. Anyway, me and Jimmy gained entry to a flat on the fifth floor. I think it belonged to a second cousin (once removed and twice locked up) of Old Tombstone. Well, nothing remarkable here – except of course for the horse that was tethered on the balcony and munching hay.

"'Ere, Jimmy, come and have a butcher's!"

"Blimey Sarge! It's a bloomin' 'orse! How do ya reckon it got here then?"

"Obvious, isn't it?"

"Is it?"

"Course it is! The horse is called Pegasus and it flew here."

"Did you ask the horse?" I said.

"Ha! Should've done. I tell you, in the end nothing I found in Melsham surprised me one little bit. It wouldn't have been anything unusual if we'd found a crocodile tucked under the bed!"

"Funny you should say that," chipped in Dr McKindlay.

"Go on," we all said together …

The London Village of Melsham (Part 3)

DeVille began the evening by introducing me to his main sources of information on the London village of Melsham. In addition to his own direct experience of the people and the place, there were a number of significant characters and informants – as it were.

Firstly, of course there was old Abraham, *Tombstone* himself, fount of all gypsy lore and very knowledgeable in criminal law too. He was Patriarch Emeritus of the village and father of half its inhabitants, apparently. He was as generous in his favours as he was careful in his responsibilities. In addition to his single front-tooth, he was distinguished by his long grey hair, worn in a ponytail, and double-hunter that he kept in his chequered waistcoat pocket, attached to a long gold chain. The watch was a symbol of his authority as well as an impressive timepiece. There was no business in Melsham that Abraham was not fully aware of, nothing that he did not sanction or otherwise cast his unrestricted retribution upon.

Secondly, there was Mr Norbert (Nobby) Clarke Q.C. of whom DeVille had this to say: "*Clarke the Shark*, we used to call him, Melsham's very own notorious Lawyer. When he ventured abroad, along the High Street to the bank, or even as far as the Magistrates Court, or very occasionally to the Old Bailey, he always wore an old-fashioned type of bowler hat. It was dark, with a felt band, and full weatherworn. It defined him. Neither one existed without the other, like a man and his shadow. Nobby Clarke, we knew, was the self-appointed Defender of both the innocent and the guilty alike, but mostly the guilty. He was sharp as a viper, and slippery as an eel. He was very good at his job. Nobby knew old Tombstone from way back in the day, when he was first apprenticed to Messrs Hurley & Burleigh (God rest their souls). And now he was sole senior partner, head of the revered scion that is now known as *Clarke & Partners (deceased)*."

And then there was Father Rupert, the local Catholic Priest. You know, Gypsy communities are typically either staunch Church of England or partisan Roman Catholic. These allegiances extend back to the Civil War, I believe. In those days the village of Melsham was decidedly Royalist. That is to say, Roman Catholic. It still is. The church building was deemed surplus to requirements, as far as the Church Commissioners were concerned, and so it was sold to the local Catholic Diocese. It became *high* church where *smells-and-bells* accompanied communal worship and elevated the individual to some higher spiritual plane apparently.

"Well, in my day," said DeVille, "Some if not all sins, were routinely confessed to Father Rupert who, as a natural consequence, held a wealth of knowledge about the inhabitants of Melsham. He was privy not only to their births, deaths, and marriages but also to their petty foibles and their venial, sometimes mortal, sins. However, whilst Nobby Clarke and Father Rupert, two venerable and variably trustworthy members of society, were bound to their own peculiar articles of *confidentiality,* the one according to Man's Law and the other according to God's, the secular and sceptical Dr McKindlay was, by contrast, somewhat less reticent about his *flock*."

This was significantly so only where non-medical matters were concerned, and of course most matters of real interest were not in fact medical at all. And now the characters were all displayed DeVille began his tale:

"Let me tell you about young Sam," he said.

"Why not," I replied, knowing he would anyway.

"Well Sam Taylor had an idea. You have to realise that ideas were very rare in a place like Melsham. Both ideas and planning were virtually unknown in the village. Instinct ruled. Mostly there were words and actions, and no original ideas or planning at all, except for where the stalls at the annual Fayre should be sited and who was selected to be in the cricket team for Saturday's match with the neighbouring rival village. These particular matters were generally agreed by tradition and convention. However, this was one of those very rare and special occasions when, by some lucky chance, or by an accidental bolt of God's own lightning that resulted in an unintended direct hit, that the quantum probability of an idea became a one hundred percent certainty. As if inspiration possessed a man! On the day in question, a fine spring day ripe with pollen, we discover that Samuel Taylor has availed himself, entirely unwittingly, of an *idea*. He has decided to offer his services to the Church, or more precisely to *St Michael and All Angels*, for the purposes of clearing the gutters and downpipes that are attached to the roof upon which the angels sometimes sit."

DeVille paused, as if requiring affirmation that he had my full attention and that I appreciated the finely balanced nature of his description, like an angel precariously perched on the church roof. I realised the simile was flawed but used it anyway.

"Go on," I said. He did.

"To achieve the aforementioned aims Sam required access to heights well beyond the reach of mere mortals, unblessed as they are without wings and the power of flight. And Sam was no angel. He called at the Presbytery and, offering to free gutters and downpipes alike, as if to cleanse them of their sins, asked to borrow a ladder. Father Rupert was only too pleased to help one of his flock carry out this holy and wholly necessary work. After all, *the Lord moves in mysterious ways, His wonders to perform.*

I remember Father Rupert telling me at the time how pleased he was and then later, much later, how naïve and stupid he felt. Over time he became more streetwise and far less easily duped. But let me get to the nub of the story. As you will have realised already, Samuel Taylor was definitely no angel but a thorough rogue. Although he had what he thought was an original idea, he didn't possess the brains to see his plan through to completion. No, it was the ladder. It was the ladder that was the cause of his downfall.

Samuel was in court. His lawyer was a certain Mr Norbert Clarke QC, learned counsel of Melsham, well known to the local Magistrates and as far afield as the Old Bailey, as you know. His lucrative cases were matters of national interest. His personal interest in the fortunes of the people of Melsham afforded him no pecuniary advantage. Rather he looked on it as a hobby, something for his own amusement, when he chose to represent the villagers in court. He performed his indiscriminate services with equal vigour and diligence in courts across the land both high and low.

Today he was in practice at the local Magistrates court. The evidence was as follows:

1. Lead flashing removed from church roof.
2. Broken ladder found in adjacent graveyard.
3. Samuel Taylor has his left arm in plaster.
4. Driver's licence is found at the bottom of a downpipe.
5. Missing tiles found in a lock-up belonging to Samuel Taylor.

The defence was straightforward:

1. The evidence was circumstantial,
2. the accident coincidental,
3. and the lead rooftiles had been found and placed in the lock-up for safe-keeping.

Unfortunately Mr Samuel Taylor had received a bump on the head (if it please the court, exhibit A) when, on the night in question, he fell down the stairs at home and broke his arm. As a consequence he suffered a temporary loss of memory and completely forgot about the church rooftiles he had discovered earlier that same evening on his way home from the pub.

The Witnesses:

4. Father Rupert confirms he commissioned Samuel Taylor to clear gutters and downpipes and that his ladder was used for the purpose,
5. He identifies the broken ladder in the churchyard is his.
6. Dr McKinlay confirms the head injury could lead to memory loss and partial or temporary *amnesia triopical.*
7. Old Abraham confirms that the ladder in question had been perfectly sound when used to put up the bunting at last year's village Fayre.

The Accused:

9. "I found the stuff. I didn't nick it!" declares Samuel Taylor.

The Gallery:

9.   "He wasn't even driving the van!" screams the defendant's mother, jumping to her feet in the gods of the public gallery.

The Magistrate:

10. "Madam, I believe the defendant is also facing another charge on an entirely different matter. That is not this case in this court at this time. If you would care to return tomorrow?"

"And did she?" I asked.

DeVille raised an eyebrow, then put it down again, together with an empty wine glass. It was time for further refreshment.

A Visit to Melsham

DeVille has suggested, if not actually insisted, I should accompany him on a tour of present day Melsham. This I have agreed to do. I think it will be useful research. Our plan is to embark on this venture in the morning, not too early but not too late. Having been born in the area, Melsham is a name that has existed on the periphery of memory ever since I can recall but I do not think I have ever been there. Except perhaps in imagination. Now it is the real thing and I am about to embark on a pilgrimage to this mythological place. DeVille will be my *Virgil*, my spiritual and literary guide, as we descend into the circles of fire and witness the everyday struggles and sufferings of humanity. I shall be Dante, if only for a day.

I take notes. I listen and observe as DeVille points out the landmarks: here is the block of flats where the pony was found, tethered on a fifth-floor balcony; there is the site of the Red House, where the pony and trap races, across the common, began. It is now a breezeblock shack with a blue plastic-sheet roof. And then there is the Blue House at the other end of the common, and the two false windows on the upper storey, and the old fire station in beautiful red brick, still standing but unused, usurped by the massive modern hanger replete with modern idle goddesses that we passed earlier, and the cricket green with its perfectly white sight-screen – the oldest cricket club in the county. We stop at the site of the old windmill, a permitted development on an acre of enclosed common way back at the beginning of the nineteenth century. There is, still preserved, with informative plaque, the base of the mill whose sails caught fire and were seen spinning like a giant Catherine wheel for miles around. We stop for a drink at the old Mill House, the *Mercer and Market*, as it is now called, another fine pub-chain establishment, staffed by youngsters of an age that we can no longer remember but instantly recognise: students, and year-outs from overseas, and learners of English *in situ*, and listeners inadvertent, enchanted by my Virgil's narrative control, his convolutions and

illusions, his voluminous and voluble word traffic, engaging, enveloping, and entrapping his unintended victims. I cannot break the spell. Meanwhile I discuss fruit and allotments and jam with the barmaid whose cocktail-wars include: strawberries and raspberries, and lemon quarters and cucumber slices. She marvels at my informative exposition on the subject of fruit and jam-making and all things – or perhaps she is just practising her listening skills. Meanwhile she attends to our drinks order and I pay contactless.

I make notes on the back of a receipt and will refer to them in due course, just to make sure I include all that was of interest, was curious, was essential from our visit to the London village of Melsham. But, while it is fresh in my mind, I will try to capture as much as possible of the flavour, of the quality, of the sincerity of the place itself. It is not as I originally imagined; it is not as rural. Or rather, it is a very odd mixture of contrasting urban and rural landscapes. Of course that is very much London as seen from the air: the great parks in the centre and the outer villages and former airfields. It also contains fine examples of contrasting buildings: those that are listed as part of an *Arts and Crafts* style con-servation area, and those that are some of the finest examples of post-war social housing. And squeezed between the two are the miniature alms houses, rendered in classic yellow London brick, the sort I recognise from a close up inspection of the crumbling mortar in a domestic property that I once assisted in re-rendering (I held the ladder) over at Crystal Palace. But it is always other than I imagined it, as if it has attained mythic proportions and is something other than the literal and my own earthly recreation.

We entered Melsham via the expansive area of common, though we were motoring along an A road. DeVille pointed out a statue of the Common's great benefactor, its guardian angel and saviour, he who had rescued it from the irreversible fate of development, of housing and parking and industrial units. I had not heard of him before but I shall remember him. Curiously his name was *Common*, George Common; inevitably apt, truth being stranger than fiction.

But it would be remiss of me if I did not mention, and give praise to, our long-suffering *chauffeuse* for the day, Narine, who endured the indefinite directions of DeVille: "straight ahead/this way, left – other left, see where that van's going? (we did not), straight on – no, the road's closed – take the next exit, here!" We have to pull over. Who's the crew driving that ambulance? Narine thinks she recognises them. She is in the W.R.V.S. and knows the crews who work in the field and report back to A&E at the local hospital.

We pass a dead-end road called *Tramway Path*. It leads down to the modern-day tram stop but formerly it led to the old trams that ran along this same route. Of course, the old trams vanished long ago, well before the trolley-buses that I still remember: the blue flashes and the smell of shorting lines and the long pole to reset the pick-up rods. I had forgotten about the poles but a chance conversation on board a modern day *Routemaster*, reminded me. We were seated upstairs at the front. I wasn't driving the bus. I checked with the gentleman to my left. No, he wasn't driving the bus either ... we trusted in the man downstairs.

We passed some picturesque period alms houses. They were quite tiny, though well proportioned, of the late Victorian or early Edwardian period I judged, a mix of Arts & Crafts and Art Nouveau styles. Nearby was a small cemetery, it was the local Commonwealth War Grave, where many sons and brothers were buried and whose names were registered on the modest concrete obelisk that stood on a round concrete plinth or dais.

Opposite the cemetery was the uniformly grey Police Station where DeVille had been based. It was a veritable Fort Apache. It was built of solid concrete, with grilled windows and crenelated walls. At each corner of the building was a watchtower complete with searchlights. It may well have been the very place where Kurt Russell was filmed in *Escape from New York*, or perhaps Steve McQueen's Stalag Luft 999 in *The Great Escape*. This was where DeVille had signed in and out, kept his locker locked and tidy, and put two sugars in his strong tea, which was poured from a large brown enamel pot by ladies with muscular arms and all-weather smiles, who served cakes and sandwiches in the canteen. This was where DeVille had variously amused and bemused the Duty Desk Sergeant. Within these walls was a temporary safe haven from the urban jungle that surrounded the last outpost of civilisation.

As we slowed down in traffic and were negotiating a left-hand bend Narine spotted something and there, trotting jauntily round the bend came a pony and trap, a typical gypsy pony with a fine blond mane, *Beatle-cut* fetlocks and a long full tail. The driver was as cool as James Bond in his Aston Martin DB5. He too sported long blond hair. And then they were gone and we were heading back towards Beckenham.

Acknowledgements

I must thank my Editor and my proof readers for all the efforts they made in trying to knock this book into shape. They have proved most assiduous in correcting my factual, grammatical and typographical mistakes. I lay claim to any errors that remain.

I would like to thank my pilot readers for their helpful comments and encouragement. I would also like to thank the landlord of the *Pig & Whistle*, who made us welcome many times at his fine hostelry. Thanks are, of course, due to all of DeVille's former colleagues who so generously shared with me the benefit of their experience and helped me sift mere fact from fiction. And finally, I would like to thank DeVille himself, without whom none of this would have been plausible. And finally the police dog, of course!

IMB
(March, 2021)
www.bundellbros.co.uk

Lightning Source UK Ltd.
Milton Keynes UK
UKHW011103210222
398997UK00002B/44